The Maxwell Manual for Good Citizenship

Public Policy Skills in Action

Bill Coplin

With the Assistance of Emily Sandefer

Maxwell School of Citizenship and Public Affairs, Syracuse University

ROWMAN & LITTLEFIELD PUBLISHERS, INC.
Lanham • Boulder • New York • Toronto • Plymouth, UK

Published by Rowman & Littlefield Publishers, Inc.
A wholly owned subsidiary of The Rowman & Littlefield Publishing Group, Inc.
4501 Forbes Boulevard, Suite 200, Lanham, Maryland 20706
http://www.rowmanlittlefield.com

Estover Road, Plymouth PL6 7PY, United Kingdom

British Library Cataloguing in Publication Information Available

ISBN 978-0-936826-44-8 (cl. : alk. Paper)

♾™ The paper used in this publication meets the minimum requirements of American
National Standard for Information Sciences—Permanence of Paper for Printed Library
Materials, ANSI/NISO Z39.48-1992.

Printed in the United States of America

About the Author

William D. Coplin is Professor of Public Affairs and Director of the Public Affairs Program of the Maxwell School at Syracuse University. As contributing author to the guidelines for the Regents twelfth grade required course (1988-89) "Participation in Government," Dr. Coplin was able to draw upon his years of teaching and expertise in public policy analysis and social science education. He has published more than 100 books and articles in the social science and political science fields. His most recent books are *How You Can Help: A Guide to Doing Good Deeds in Your Everyday Life* (2000), *Ten Things Employers Want You to Learn in College* (2003) and *25 Ways to Make College Pay Off: Advice for Anxious Parents from a Professor Who's Seen it All* (2007). In addition, over the past few years, he has written articles for *USA-Today* and the *Chronicle of Higher Education*.

Professor Coplin, who received his Ph.D. from American University, has received numerous teaching awards from Syracuse University, including the Laura J. and L. Douglas Meredith Professorship for Teaching Excellence. In addition, he is the founder and director of the undergraduate Policy Studies program at Syracuse University. This manual is the basic text for PAF 101: Introduction to the Analysis of Public Policy, is the gateway course to the Policy Studies major, which prepares its graduates to do good and do well after college.

Acknowledgements

This manual draws from the third edition of *Public Policy Skills*, which I co-authored with a colleague at the Maxwell School, Michael K. O'Leary. Dr. O'Leary, who passed away in 2003, received his Ph.D. from Princeton University. He taught at Princeton and at the University of Southern California and Dartmouth College before becoming a faculty member at the Maxwell School in 1965.

The manual has benefited greatly from reactions and constructive criticism to the three editions of *Public Policy Skills* used in PAF 101: Introduction to the Analysis of Public Policy by more than 2,500 students at Syracuse University and more than 10,000 students at high schools who take this course and earn Syracuse University credit. Even more valued have been the comments of an extremely talented and dedicated set of high school teachers throughout New York State who have worked closely with us in Syracuse University's Project Advance Program. They have made many of the revisions that led to this manual based on their experiences teaching the course.

Several of these teachers served on a book development committee over the past two years to suggest changes and revisions to the book. These teachers are Karen Bonventre of Shenendehowa, Barbara Heller of East Syracuse Minoa, Phil Rudolph of Fayetteville Manlius, Michelle Gosh of Brewster, and Gary Moran of Wantagh. The committee was formed by Pat Gallagher, a former teacher at Seaford High School, and now a teacher trainer and faculty supervisor for the Project Advance courses. Pat has been a driving force for the change in title and approach that has transformed the original text into a dynamic manual.

John Fiset, who is the administrator for Project Advance, has provided the resources, encouragement, and insight to shape this manual. His commitment to a quality education for our students has been instrumental in completing the manuscript.

Michael Pasqualoni, Public Administration and Instructional Services Librarian at Syracuse University, who has given lectures to my class, drafted Chapter 2 to accommodate the momentous changes that have occurred in information sources over the past decade.

My editorial assistant and manuscript developer, Emily Sandefer, played a crucial role in developing this book. She added content where it was needed, revised the writing throughout the book, and was a constant source of motivation to me. Without her, this book would not have been written.

Table of Contents

Introduction

"Teaching Democracy in the abstract is like trying to teach someone to swim by correspondence."
— John Dewey

If you have bought this manual for PAF 101, DO NOT SELL IT AFTER THIS CLASS!

I say this for four reasons:

1. When you buy your first home and the city wants to build a garbage dump next to it, this manual will refresh your skills to fight this injustice.

2. When you want to make the world a better place, this manual will refresh the skills you need to work toward it in a constructive way.

3. When you vote or participate in the political process in some other way, this manual will refresh the skills you need to keep the politicians working for the public good rather than themselves.

4. When you embark on a career, this manual will refresh the skills you need to go as far as you want.

There is one other reason why you should not sell this manual. If you sell it, you will be contributing to the corruption of the used book market. They buy the book back from you at 20 percent of the price you paid and sell it to other students for 80 percent of the original sale price. Because of the used book market, publishers keep publishing new editions of almost the same book, which raises the costs for everyone. They have a right to make a profit, but the used book market is why you pay such outrageous prices for books. With no public policy to fix this problem, book publishers will continue to gouge college students.

While we are on this subject, every cent of the royalties for this book is donated to the Public Affairs Program of the Maxwell School of Syracuse University to provide financial support for undergraduates on projects to make the world better.

I hope that I have made it clear that this manual is not your typical textbook. There are no terms to memorize but only terms to use. There is no factual information for you to master but only skills to acquire in order to apply them in your life. This manual demands your action in order for you to learn. Your active participation in the exercises and activities associated with the book will make you a smarter student. More importantly, if you work hard enough on its message, you will become a better person in your relationships with others, in your career, and as a citizen.

You are inheriting a world that needs good citizens: people who do good but also do well. America needs its citizens to support themselves through hard work and creativity and to protect the democracy from destructive forces within and outside the country.

A lot of books and people will tell you that learning how to be a good citizen is a matter of studying the Constitution, reading the Federalist papers, or studying American history. While understanding the foundation and history of your country is important, it is not the most important way to become a good citizen. The most important ingredients of good citizenship are the **skills** and **character** you use to protect your own self-interest and to enhance the public interest; to carve out a place in the economy to help yourself; and to take actions to help others. You will see how these ingredients of good citizenship are integrated in the course objectives which are listed below:

1. Become willing and able to "do good" effectively.

2. Define and identify the components of public policy issues.

3. Communicate ideas and findings with respect to public policy issues.

4. Collect information on public policy issues.

5. Use graphs, tables, and statistics to analyze public policy.

6. Examine the use of surveys and informal interviewing procedures.

7. Identify a social problem and come up with a proposed public policy to deal with it.

8. List the benefits and costs of a proposed public policy.

9. Develop benchmarks to assess the impact of your policy on societal conditions.

10. Analyze the political factors and develop strategies to implement a proposed public policy.

11. Identify essential features of major current public policy issues.

12. Work in teams effectively.

You should look at this manual as training for action. At the end of the course, you will write a policy memo to a player suggesting that he or she accept your policy recommendation. The memo will be professional and will have both the format and content that politicians and government officials use in the real world.

As far as the skills go, I have identified a comprehensive list of 38 essential skills in my widely read book, *10 Things Employers Want You to Learn in College.* The table on the next page provides you a list of the 38 skills. You already have many of them, but you must always seek a higher level. The skills are not just the skills you need to get an A in your school work. Many of them will help you do that and be a much better student. But even more important than helping with your grades, these skills will put you on a road to find and achieve the American Dream as well as to help others do the same.

You will be able to practice every one of these skills through the course with the help of this manual. Remember that you never "have" the skills; you only have the ability to perform the skills in whatever you do. You may have a good day or a bad day, so always work to continuously improve your skills. As Aristotle said, "We are what we repeatedly do. Excellence, then, is not an act, but a habit." Good citizenship is about excellence.

Good citizenship is also about doing good. In the main entrance to the Maxwell School at Syracuse University, as you can see on the back cover of this manual, a statue of George Washington stands in front of a very important statement, the Athenian Oath. The key sentence in the Oath is: "…we will transmit this City, not only not less, but greater and more beautiful than it was transmitted to us." Good citizens make things better not just for their family and friends but for the neighborhood, town, city, county, state, country, and world which has sustained their lives.

A Word about Maxwell in the Title: This manual has been used to teach more than 30,000 students at Syracuse University and in a college credit course taught at more than 50 high schools as part of the academic program of the Maxwell School of Citizenship and Public Affairs. Rated the Number 1 school of public affairs in the country by *U.S. News and World Report* since 1995, the Maxwell School is the only school in the country with the word "citizenship" in its title. The Maxwell School is also the oldest school in the country that prepares people for public service with government and non-profit agencies. The hallmark of the Maxwell School is a combination of the idealism embodied in the Athenian Oath and training to be a professional in all walks of life. Using this book and taking a course based on it prepares you to bring your heart and your mind to solving the many problems that we face in the twenty-first century.

Skills for Any Professional Career

Establishing a Work Ethic
>Kick Yourself in the Butt • Be Honest • Manage Your Time • Manage Your Money

Developing Physical Skills
>Stay Well • Look Good • Type 35 WPM Error Free • Take Legible Notes

Communicating Verbally
>Converse One-on-One • Present to Groups • Use Visual Displays

Communicating in Writing
>Write Well • Edit and Proof • Use Word-Processing Tools • Send Information Electronically

Working Directly with People
>Build Good Relationships • Work in Teams • Teach Others

Influencing People
>Manage Efficiently • Sell Successfully • Politick Wisely • Lead Effectively

Gathering Information
>Use Library Holdings • Use Commercial Databases • Search the Web • Conduct Interviews • Use Surveys • Keep and Use Records

Using Quantitative Tools
>Use Numbers • Use Graphs and Tables • Use Spreadsheet Programs

Asking and Answering the Right Questions
>Detect BS • Pay Attention to Detail • Apply Knowledge • Evaluate Actions and Policies

Solving Problems
>Identify Problems • Develop Solutions • Launch Solutions

Based on Bill Coplin's *10 Things Employers Want You to Learn in College* (Ten Speed Press, 2003).

Supplementary Materials on Website: Instructors can have students download the exercises and place them in a word processing file so they can be completed as assignments to the book. The PAF 101 homepage can be found at http://classes.maxwell.syr.edu/paf101. The homepage is updated frequently and maintained under the Maxwell School of Citizenship and Public Affairs at Syracuse University. At this website you will find tips and other recommendations on developing public policy skills as well as lists of research sites and guidelines for APA (American Psychological Association) style.

Instructors and students are also advised to spend some time searching a website the author has created for doing good and doing well at http://www.maxwell.syr.edu/paf. This site provides materials to motivate and educate students to develop their skills and character so they can enjoy the benefits of living in America and at the same time work to improve the vision embodied in the Declaration of Independence.

Profile of a Global Citizen

John Dau

Each chapter ends with a description of the activities of someone who has used the skills and demonstrated the character that you will develop during this semester. Let me introduce you to our first person, John Dau. John is one of the Lost Boys of Sudan who settled in Syracuse after escaping from government troops who wanted to kill him and other people in southern Sudan. He spent 13 years walking through the desert and living in refugee camps. Murder and starvation were all around him. At 12 years old, he was in charge of more than 1,000 children in the refugee camps. He came to America in 2001 and worked 60 hours a week in a job as a security guard, bought a house, wrote a book with another writer, and gave speeches throughout the country. In addition, he established a foundation to obtain money and build a health clinic in his home country of Sudan. He is proud to be an American, but he is dedicated to helping people from the country of his birth.

Chapter 1

Three Essential Components for Public Policy Analysis and Action

"Be ashamed to die until you have won some victory for Humanity."
— Horace Mann, in a commencement address at Antioch College in 1859

YOUR GOAL   To apply the definitions of societal problems, public policies, and players.

Introduction

To get a picture of what public policy analysis and action mean, let us say a group of students in your class conducts what we call the Team Policy Exercise. In this exercise, you go through the following steps:

1. Determine what is wrong with your school. Perhaps you think it is poor food in the cafeteria, or teachers who are not doing a good job, or too many students who fail to graduate. Whatever the problem, identifying it is the first step in the analysis.

2. Conduct research by collecting information from various sources including students, teachers, administrators, books, articles, and websites.

3. Come up with a policy that will reduce the problem. For example, if the problem is poor cafeteria food, your policy could be to hire an outside company to provide the food. If the problem is poor teaching, your policy could be to conduct and publish course surveys.

4. Discuss why you think your policy will be effective. **Effective** means that the policy reduces the problem. For example, an outside company might produce better food because it has to satisfy students or it will lose its contract with the school district. Or teachers seeing their course evaluations made public will want to put more effort into doing a better job.

5. Discuss why you think the policy would be feasible. **Feasible** means the likelihood that those in power will actually implement the policy. For example, you might say that bringing in an outside firm for food services would face opposition, but if current workers were hired by the firm, it might have a chance. On the policy to publish course evaluations of teachers, you might say it would not be feasible because the teachers' union would object.

The Team Policy Exercise can be attempted at any time. It is a good thing to try because it introduces you to all the aspects of public policy analysis. If you try it at the beginning of the course, you will see how difficult the process is and how it is necessary to develop a lot of important skills. By the end of the course, you will be able to do a much better job and come up with a policy proposal that you can actually present to real world players.

The Maxwell Manual introduces you to three key components of public policy analysis. Each of these components requires you to learn some specific words that you should use whenever you think about or discuss public policy. Although you need to learn the definitions of these words, it is more important that you practice using the words in a way that is true to their meaning. As you read this chapter, try to apply them. In the list below, you will see that there are only 11 specific words or phrases you need to use to begin your analysis of any public policy or societal problem. Master the use of these words and you will be well on your way to becoming a solid public policy analyst.

The three components of public policy are:

1. Identifying societal problems (Key words: societal problems, levels of government, federal, state, local)

2. Identifying public policy (Key words: public policy, legislative, executive/administrative, judicial)

3. Identifying players (Key words: players, stakeholders)

Component 1: Identifying Societal Problems

A societal problem exists when something is "wrong" with some aspect of society. But how do you decide if something is wrong? To decide if something is wrong, you must first decide what you think the goals of a society should be, and then determine the degree to which societal conditions further these goals. Societal problems exist if societal conditions do not further these goals.

In carrying out your first step, deciding what the goals of society should be, you do not have to look very far. The goals can be found in the Declaration of Independence: "life, liberty, and the pursuit of happiness." These are "unalienable rights" that Thomas Jefferson used in order to justify the American colonies' decision to break away from England. We will use this phrase as the guide to goals in identifying societal problems.

The terms "life," "liberty," and the "pursuit of happiness" need to be explained in more detail to provide a comprehensive guide to identifying societal problems.

Life: People want to enjoy good health and avoid the dangers of diseases, pollutants, and malnutrition. People would also like to enjoy personal safety unthreatened by foreign attack, street crime, unsafe roads, or dangerous products.

Liberty: People want to freely express themselves regarding politics, religion, and culture. They also want to be free to choose where they live, with whom they associate, and the style of life they lead.

Pursuit of happiness: This broad range of concerns can be grouped under two headings. First, economic opportunity should be open to **all** and should be in sufficient quantity to allow people to survive and enjoy themselves. Second, a clean physical environment is required for good health as well as personal satisfaction.

Making judgments about societal conditions relates to the six goals. A balance needs to be struck among the six goals because the extreme pursuit of one may reduce the amount achieved regarding another. For example, free expression that would allow someone to falsely yell "fire" in a crowded theater would reduce the personal safety of those in the theater. A society dedicated to an excessively clean environment may find reduced freedom of choice because of strict regulation.

Figure 1.1: Six Societal Goals

Life	Liberty	Pursuit of Happiness
1. Good Health	3. Free expression	5. Economic opportunity
2. Personal Safety	4. Free choice	6. Clean environment

Whose Problem?

A **societal problem** is when some aspect of our society, or, as we will call it, "a societal condition," fails to meet one or more of the six goals. Of course, people interpret societal problems differently. For example, a societal problem for undergraduates at many universities and colleges is the number of closed courses. A closed class reduces the freedom of choice for the student and may even threaten the student's chances for economic opportunity. It is a pervasive problem that most directly affects undergraduates. Faculty, graduate students, and administrators may not see the number of closed courses as a serious problem. They may even argue that students avoid taking courses early in the morning or late in the afternoon, which is why so many of the chosen courses are closed. The seriousness of the problem, therefore, depends on whose view is considered. However, if the number of closed classes leads to a situation in which undergraduates cannot register for a full schedule or are forced to attend summer school, other groups may agree that it is in fact a societal problem.

For this reason, when you define a societal problem, you also need to discuss which groups are most affected by the problem and which of the six goals are being threatened. Some groups will always feel more intensely than others about the seriousness of a societal problem. In addition, groups look at the problems from the perspective of different goals. When you study societal problems, you need to be aware of these differences.

One final point: you must bring your own individual perspective to the application of the six goals. This book is not intended to make you an effective lobbyist for a specific group. One goal of this book is that you act to improve societal conditions. You should be aware of the legitimate preferences of others, but even more importantly, you must decide which societal problems are most important from your own perspective as someone who accepts the goals outlined in the Declaration of Independence.

Where Is the Problem?

Problems can be dealt with at different levels of government. The location of a societal problem also needs to be carefully considered. Figure 1.2 lists the names of the legislative, executive/administrative, and judicial branches at each level of government (national, state, and local).

Figure 1.3 illustrates the roles of the three elements of public policy (legislation, executive/administrative acts, and judicial decisions) at three levels of government in the United States (local, state, and national) with respect to the distribution of the flu vaccine. Think of additional examples that could fit in each box for other topics that you read about or hear about.

Figure 1.2: Levels and Branches of Government

	Legislative	Executive/ Administrative	Judicial
National	Congress	President (plus Cabinet and administrative departments)	U.S. Supreme Court U.S. Court of Appeals U.S. District Courts
State	Assembly and Senate (for NY, but differs by state)	Governor (plus administrative departments)	State Courts (differs by state, but generally follows same structure as national level)
Local	City Council/ Common Council (may be called something else)	Mayor	Local Courts (many different types, like family court, surrogates court)
School Board	Board of Education	Superintendent	Would revert to local courts

Analyzing a societal problem involves identifying the primary location of the problem. Are you concerned with the problem in your own community or at the state or national level? What level of government makes the decision? You will also eventually need to look at the interdependence between the primary location and other locations; what happens internationally and nationally frequently affects states and local communities.

Selecting a location or level of government will depend upon the availability of information as well as the purpose of your analysis. If you want to do something about the problem, you will probably need to work in a local community. If you want to obtain a broader view of the problem or you are completing a study for a

Figure 1.3: Levels of Government and Types of Action

	Legislation	Executive/ Administrative Acts	Judicial Decisions
Local	County establishes a program to distribute flu vaccine	Allocate funds and appoint staff for the clinic	Citizens might claim vaccine damaged their health
State	State legislates budget allocation to counties	Department of Health decides how much funding each county gets	Citizens might claim vaccine damaged their health
National	Federal government requires county to set up clinics	Center for Disease Control approves vaccine	Citizens might claim vaccine damaged their health

course, you may want to study the state or national dimensions of the problem. You also need to consider what level of government has the authority to make decisions about the problem.

Component 2: Identifying Public Policy

A **public policy** is an actual or proposed government action intended to deal with a given societal problem. An example of a public policy is the New York State law which changed the drinking age from 19 to 21. There are three elements of government actions:

Legislation: The legislative aspect of public policy establishes guidelines to be followed by members of the society. A law raising the drinking age from 19 to 21 is intended to stop 19 and 20 year olds from consuming alcoholic beverages. Notice that a law does not necessarily mean that people will behave differently. Governments cannot make people do anything; they can only tell them what is legal behavior and punish them if they act illegally.

Executive/Administrative Acts: Executive/administrative acts are what governments do to put a law into practice. They include such actions as: mailing social security checks; giving tickets to people who illegally park their cars; or scheduling when trash will be collected. These acts are often even more important than the laws themselves. For example, if the police decide not to vigorously enforce the legal drinking age, the law will have little effect on those under 21.

Judicial Decisions: Judicial decisions take place when courts apply the law to a specific situation. They may have the effect of both executive/administrative and legislative acts. For example, existing laws may be declared unconstitutional. The legal situation then returns to the situation that existed prior to the passage of the law. Furthermore, judges may issue sentences to law violators in ways that either increase or decrease the force of the law. For example, since the early 1980s, violators of drunk driving laws have received harsher penalties, in part, because of stricter judicial decisions.

All three types of government actions are required for any public policy. The legislature of the state enacts legislation defining a crime; the executive branch administers the law by arresting and prosecuting the defendant; and the state court determines whether the defendant is guilty of the crime.

Sometimes, government actions are not so simple. For example, to reduce the number of highway accidents, a state sets speed limits on its roads. Making and carrying out such policies involves legislation, executive/administrative acts, and judicial decisions. The legislature of the state enacts general legislation; the Department of Transportation in the state determines the actual limit for a particular stretch of road and the police patrol the road and give tickets to speeders. Finally, the local courts decide on penalties for violators of the law.

Component 3: Identifying Players and Stakeholders

Players: Individuals, groups, or institutions that work to influence public policies. Players can be elected officials, appointed officials, organized citizen groups, civic associations, industry trade groups, or private individuals who seek to shape policy.

Stakeholders: Individuals and groups who are affected by the activities of an organization and therefore have a stake in them. Unorganized categories of people such as the public, voters, consumers, and taxpayers are stakeholders because they are affected by public policies.

All players are stakeholders because they are affected by public policies. Players have a stake in the policies that are made by their organizations, because these policies can affect their power. However, not all stakeholders are players. Stakeholders do not have power over the policies that are made by organizations.

Applying the Three Components of Public Policy Issues

You have now been introduced to the three essential components of a public policy issue. Figure 1.4 on the next page outlines how these three components interrelate.

This diagram is a general outline for thinking about topics in this book. Societal problems motivate players to call for public policies that, in turn, affect the societal problem. When analyzing any public policy issue, you should be able to identify the public policy, the societal problem, the players, and the relationship among the three components. Always ask yourself the three questions suggested by Arrows 1, 2, and 3 in Figure 1.4:

1. What is the expected impact of the public policy on the societal problem *[Arrow 1]*?

2. Which players support and which players oppose the public policy *[Arrow 2]*?

3. How does the societal problem stimulate the behavior of players *[Arrow 3]*?

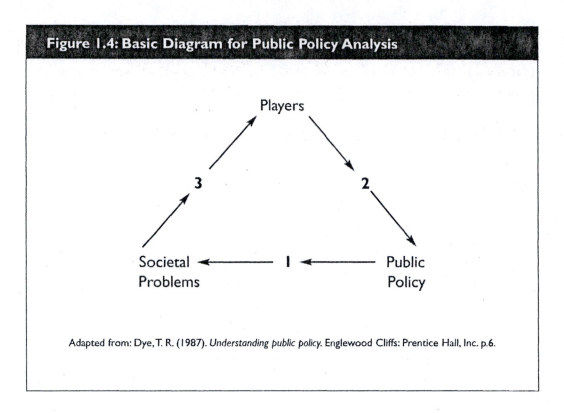

Figure 1.4: Basic Diagram for Public Policy Analysis

Players

3   2

Societal ← I ← Public
Problems   Policy

Adapted from: Dye, T. R. (1987). *Understanding public policy.* Englewood Cliffs: Prentice Hall, Inc. p.6.

For example, here is how the three arrows from Figure 1.4 apply to a national speed limit.

Arrow 1: The intended or actual impact of a public policy on the societal problems. For example, the 55 miles per hour speed limit reduces gasoline consumption and cuts down on traffic fatalities.

Arrow 2: The position of a player on a public policy. For example, the AAA favors the 55 miles per hour speed limit.

Arrow 3: Societal problems motivate players to support or oppose this public policy. For example, a massive increase in the price of oil in the mid-1970s motivated Congress to implement the 55 miles per hour speed limit. The rise in oil prices in 2005 and 2006 has not led to the same action.

Selecting a Public Policy Topic

Throughout the remainder of the manual, you will study one public policy topic in depth. You will be given a series of tasks in each chapter to enhance your skills of public policy analysis. To properly develop these skills, you will need to become as knowledgeable as possible about your topic. Although your instructor may allow you to switch topics, it will generally be easier for you to do a good job if you keep the same topic throughout. Keeping the same topic throughout will allow you to become an expert on the topic. Therefore, think carefully about what will interest you, what you are capable of understanding, and your capacity to acquire the necessary information. Here are some questions you should ask yourself to help make a good choice:

1. What societal problem am I deeply concerned about and why?

2. At what level of government (local, state, national) should I focus in my study?

3. Do I have any background on the subject?

4. Do I know some people who are players and/or experts, or have contacts with players and/or experts whom I might contact?

5. Will I be able to apply Figure 1.4 to my choice? That is, am I sure that I have clearly defined a societal problem; do I have some idea of at least one of the major players and/or experts; and can I think of at least one existing or proposed public policy?

Profile of A Policy-Maker

Wendy Kopp

Because this is a manual and a course to help you actually take action, your study should help you decide on a public policy that you would actually work to achieve. Just to show you how someone close to your age can make a major difference in improving society, consider Wendy Kopp, who founded Teach for America. In her senior thesis at Princeton University, using the same kind of analysis you are learning in this course, Ms. Kopp came up with the idea of a national teaching corps to reduce the problem presented by the lack of teachers willing to work in poverty-stricken areas. She raised millions of dollars and started the program in 1990 with 500 placements. In 2006, over 19,000 applied and 2,400 were selected. Since 1990, more than 20,000 teachers have served and over 60 percent have remained in teaching beyond their initial commitment. Many of the rest continue to raise funds and support in many ways the mission of Teach for America. Not only did Ms. Kopp help to reduce one of America's most serious societal problems, but she also changed public policy in cities and in the federal government. Several school districts in cities like New York, Washington, D.C., and Boston have adopted Ms. Kopp's model, and the federal government has provided funds to support the organization through AmeriCorps. Learn more about Teach for America at www.teachforamerica.org.

Chapter 2

Getting Information from Published Sources

"Knowledge is power." — Francis Bacon

YOUR GOAL   To learn how to locate and evaluate published information on your public policy issue.

Introduction

You have probably heard the quote under the title of this chapter before. It actually is wrong on two accounts. First, the word "information" should replace "knowledge" because "knowledge" implies permanent information, and things always change. Second, information can become power only if you can get it and use it. Information is like a car. If you cannot remember where you parked it and you do not know how to drive, you cannot use it. This chapter and the next two are about finding information. The rest of the book is about using it.

Gathering information is an essential task in the analysis of public policies. It presents a very big challenge for several reasons:

- The amount of information you can use is virtually unlimited.

- Many skills are necessary to access the right information and these skills can take years to develop.

- Much of the information you may locate is wrong, outdated, or not related in any way to the societal problems and public policies you want to study.

- Getting your hands on the right information may even require that you pay money to gain access to some of the information.

- To obtain and critically evaluate useful information on a topic, you already have to have some basic knowledge about that topic.

This chapter will introduce you to gathering published information. The term "published" information is used to mean any information that a publishing company, government agency, or non-profit organization makes available to the public in print or online via the Internet. The next two chapters will introduce you to gathering information from people. Like all of the skills in this book, continuous practice and experience will make you skillful in obtaining such information. This chapter merely serves as an introduction.

Good Sources

In your search for information online, be especially sensitive to any report, statistical data, or other information that appears wildly out of date. Web pages that may seem helpful at first glance but that have not been updated in months or even years are common.

Finding out if any given piece of information is both accurate and comprehensive can be time-consuming if not impossible. The best you can do is to find sources in which you have some confidence. You can never find the absolute truth, but you can take steps to make sure you are not accepting something that is not truthful. The following three steps should prove helpful.

First, you can see if the information you find is clear and makes sense according to what you already know. If you read a statistic that says 80 percent of students in your school system graduate on time, but you know that the national statistic for all school systems in the United States is 60 percent, you should be skeptical. Unless you have reason to believe your school system is way above average, you should double check with another source.

Second, you can make a judgment about the reputation of the source. Here is a series of questions to ask:

- How long have the publishers of the information been in existence? Are they a university press or major publishing company rather than a clearinghouse for unedited, self-published information?

- Are authors of the information recognized experts, and what are their affiliations?

- Does the publication describe careful editing procedures about articles it publishes?

- Is this publication referred to with respect by other publications with a longer history?

- Even if the publication is quite obscure, is this simply because it is new or targets a narrow, specialized audience?

- Is the information riddled with typographical errors, filled with broken hypertext links, or otherwise lacking rigorous publication standards?

Government publications can usually be trusted more than other sources. The information on the Internet through Google-type searches is always open to question compared to publications available from commercial databases, which we will discuss below. Websites that publish information from politicians, lobby groups, and interest groups can be truthful, but be on the lookout for bias when groups give only selected information to support their positions.

Third, the most reliable way to assess the quality of information is to seek multiple sources on the same fact. If there is a similar piece of information from three different sources, you can have more confidence than if it is from one source. Even so, you have to be concerned that the second and third source merely copied it from the first source.

A special form of seeking multiple sources that is widely used by academics involves what is called a "peer review process." Before an article is published, experts in the field are asked to review it. This process usually results in the publication of articles with fewer mistakes, but it has several downsides. First, the process takes a long time, so the material is sometimes out of date. Second, because a group of peers frequently may agree only on limited types of articles, the articles tend to be less innovative than they might be otherwise. Third, peer reviewed articles are very specialized and frequently highly theoretical which limits their usefulness in the study of many current public policy questions.

This discussion should make it clear that finding good information is always a challenge. That is why we have universities, governments, journalists, scientists, and think tanks always researching everything. You have limited time and resources to check into your sources, but as a public policy analyst and activist, you must always question the information you receive.

Citations

Whenever words, ideas, or facts are taken from somewhere other than your own mind or from clearly established sets of common knowledge, they must be cited. You should not present the information originating in the writing of others as if it were your own. There are specific formats in which sources should be cited. The style is different for just about every type of source and also depends on the professional or academic discipline you are working in, but, in general, good citations should include:

- Author

- Title

- Title of Larger Work (*a periodical title containing an article you cite*)

- Volume Number (*for a periodical article*)

- Issue Number (*for a periodical article*)

- Place of Publication (*for a book, but not an article*)

- Publishing Company (*for a book, but not an article*)

- Year of Publication

- Page Numbers (*for a periodical article*)

- Retrieved Date (*for an online source*)

- URL (*such as: http://www.genuinedogooder.com for an online source*)

This book requires the APA (American Psychological Association) style. Mastering all aspects of APA citation style or any similar style takes time, but you can get assistance if you consider one or more of the following steps:

- Visit an online guide to APA style such as those provided by:

  - Purdue University's Online Writing Lab http://owl.english. purdue.edu/owl/resource/560/01/

  - American Psychological Association's "Frequently Asked Questions" web page http://www.apastyle.org/faqs.html

- Many books on writing have simplified versions of the APA style, and you may have one in your possession. You can use them, although they may not cover all citation types.

- Borrow or purchase a copy of the most recent edition of the *Publication Manual of the American Psychological Association.* Washington, D.C.: American Psychological Association.

- Visit the reference collection of a nearby academic or public library. They typically offer various helpful print and online guides for citing sources.

- Look carefully at other published articles from journals that cite their sources according to APA style. These can be excellent models.

Recognize that citing sources is not merely a required, mechanical exercise. It is also an important part of the wider research you conduct on your public policy topic. Recent newspaper headlines are filled with stories of students and seasoned authors found to have plagiarized from other authors, sometimes because of honest failures to carefully keep track of information within their writing that is not original to them. Plagiarism penalties can be severe. Proper citation practice will help you avoid this trouble within your own written work. It will help others evaluate the policy arguments you make, allowing them to separate out your thoughts from arguments and other data you borrow directly from outside sources. Even if you restate that outside information in your own words, you must cite it. In addition, especially when just beginning to understand your topic, the formal citations to additional sources you find within bibliographies of various books and articles are extremely helpful gateways that may lead you toward finding more in-depth information about your topic.

How to Get Started on Your Information Search

How do you get started? The first step is to select a topic that interests you or your community. Like an athlete choosing a favorite sport, you increase chances of success if you work on something that is a good fit for you. Perhaps you or a family member has been affected by a policy, or perhaps you have always wondered about something. By being interested, you will naturally be motivated to seek out more information. At the very least, you should have interest and some knowledge in how your school is run, so you could choose a school problem. If you have no interests in any policy topic, you should not be reading this book or taking this course.

Second, you could scan newspapers for discussions of your policy topic, or consider policy related discussion you hear on the radio and view on television. To see what is being written about your topic online, you can do an internet search—e.g., Google or Yahoo—to get a basic feel. Google searches are good because they always produce information; they are not always so good because the information is likely to be irrelevant or extremely biased. But it is not a bad place to start when you are first brainstorming. See more on Google searches later in this chapter.

Third, ask an individual who you know or a friend of yours who will talk to you about the topic. This person may be the one who gave you the idea in the first place. Talk it over with your friends. Everybody has an opinion, and these conversations will force you to start seriously thinking about the topic.

Fourth, start thinking about your topic in a broad way. If you are interested in investigating more about underage drinking and car accidents, broaden your initial search to drinking and driving generally. It is easier to find information on general topics, and you can always narrow down your topic to a more specific topic. If you are interested in the topic of the spread of AIDS, it is better to start with the spread of all sexually transmitted diseases. As you become more knowledgeable about the general topic, it will be easier for you to find material on specific topics.

Information Gathering Tools

Once you have completed these four introductory steps, you are ready to get down to serious business by using computer-based search systems. In many cases, these search systems can be helpful tools. They may sometimes be referred to as "databases." They may also involve free search engines like Google or Yahoo, online catalogs, or commercial database systems provided at a nearby academic or public library. You will be introduced to specific lists of these later in this chapter.

Computerized search systems are not all of equal quality, even if their search screens look similar. Here are some tips you should use when selecting one or more computerized searching tools to use as part of your overall information gathering process:

1. Look for databases and other search engines that provide both basic and advanced choices for combining different search terms pertinent to your topic.

2. Do not be in such a hurry to get results that you fail to explore these advanced options. They are often not on the first screen you see when entering that system.

3. Compare how your results differ with and without the use of these advanced search features. For instance, when inside a database, you might test your ability to:

   a. Limit results to information that appears only in newspaper sources or magazines, instead of academic journals.

   b. Limit search results to information published on a specific day or during a selected time period (e.g., most recent two years).

As you use one or more computer-based search engines or online databases, your results will vastly improve if the published information these databases contain is indexed according to various subjects. What is an index? When applied to database searching, it is a form of specialized list that associates specific subject words with the individual published documents within that database. Databases can be indexed according to other factors as well. Indexing can be used to identify all documents that discuss a specific geographic location or the name of a specific person, government agency, or company. You are probably already familiar with back of book indexing. That form of indexing lists alphabetically the important names and other subject words appearing within that book and identifies the pages on which discussion of those terms appears.

The indexing used inside computer-based search systems is an important organizational feature that can help you locate pertinent information. Without it, locating a magazine or newspaper article discussing your topic is a little like attempting to locate a food item inside a large supermarket where none of the aisles contain written descriptions of the types of food on those shelves. Likewise, as you hunt for information on the Internet, the irrelevant material you encounter when entering the typical Google search happens because that enormous system is not truly indexing its web pages by topic, but only according to the individual words and phrases those pages contain. Think about it. Not every web page, nor written article, that mentions the word "drive" will also discuss "automobiles." Some of those pages will be about the subject of golf or hammering nails.

Therefore, having awareness of the indexing of subject terms is an important skill when using any computer-based search system like a database you access at a library's website. Here are six steps you can follow to make the best use of the subject indexing found in most databases:

1. Write down several different words or short phrases to describe your topic. For instance, if you are looking for articles on world hunger, you might come up with terms such as hunger, food supplies, famine, and drought. Writing these down may also lead you to recall related terms like rainfall, climate, and weather.

2. Once you have identified and written down six to ten words or short phrases, look through the available subject headings in the search system you are using to see if any of those words appear.

3. To locate the system's subject heading terms, look for a portion of that search engine, online catalog, or database that allows you to browse "subjects," "subject headings," or "descriptors" ("descriptors" are another specialized way of saying "subject").

4. Some systems provide hints for locating their lists of subject words and phrases by inserting a small image alongside the search window where subject terms are typed in (e.g., a little book, an image of a magnifying glass, or a link labeled "subjects"). If you see one of these, click on it to access the system's list of preferred subject heading terms.

5. Explore whether the search system you are using allows you to narrow your results by searching only inside specified segments (i.e., search "fields") of a document within that system. For instance, a newspaper database may allow you to limit your results according to words appearing only in the introductory paragraph of an article or in that article's title or headline. Other systems allow you to limit the results of your search to words appearing in the summary of an article, the "abstract."

6. If you get lost, try clicking on the "help" link within the search engine or database you are using to determine how to browse or search by subject headings related to your topic or to learn more about advanced search methods available within that system.

Exploring Specific Sources Used in Public Policy Research

You have completed the initial steps in your information gathering process once you have done some brainstorming to select a topic, looked for discussion of the topic in newspapers and online, discussed it with friends or family, considered broader aspects of that topic, and familiarized yourself with one or more computer-based search tools. You should now have a set of questions that you are ready to ask about the problem and the policy and a short list of subject terms about that topic. When you have these firmly in mind, you should be prepared to use the following types of sources. The remainder of this chapter will discuss these categories:

- Internet Sources
- Quantitative Data
- Newspapers
- Magazines and Journals
- Books
- United States Government Publications
- Non-Governmental Policy Publications
- United States Census Data

Internet Sources

Sometimes you will be able to find relevant information on your topic by using a search engine like Google. Although this can be the fastest way to obtain information, you need to know how to get good information from a Google search. Much like our previous discussion about searching databases, Google also offers "advanced" search options. For instance, one can use Google's advanced search page to limit results to online sources that contain a specific phrase or combination of words. When inside Google, take a look at the "About Google" link for tips on how to conduct advanced searches.

How Google Works

Before you ever type your query, Google has already visited most of the popular sites on the Internet, asked for a copy of the site, and downloaded the pages into a document database (for smaller sites, owners can tell Google to add them to its database). Google then scans the document and sends relevant terms to an index server—it does not index words like *the, is,* or *that.* When you perform a search, Google looks through its enormous index for the pages that contain matches to your search terms. These matches are organized according to their "PageRank." The first result you see when your search is done is the page with the highest PageRank, then the second highest, and so on. Hundreds of variables are used to compute the PageRank, but some of the most important include traffic to the page and how many sites link to that page.

Since there are so many variables used to determine which sites are given priority in a Google search, your search will most likely result in a great deal of material that is irrelevant to your topic. One of the greatest weaknesses of Google searching is its lack of indexing by subject. This can frequently lead you to online sources that mention words about a topic without discussing that topic in detail. Google searching is certainly a powerful research tool, but Google searching alone is rarely sufficient when gathering information about a public policy topic.

Keep in mind that some of the web pages you find using Google may often refer to other published sources without providing you free access to the full content of those sources. Advice for locating these other types of information appears in the remaining portions of this chapter. Finally, when reviewing information located online, remember to apply the principles about finding good sources discussed earlier in this chapter.

Quantitative Data

Quantitative data is crucial to exploring the societal problems you wish to study. Incorporating quantitative data into your research process will help you with precisely identifying problems as well as exploring potential causes of those problems. You can find such data from many sources, including those discussed in subsequent sections of this chapter. At advanced levels, research libraries at colleges and universities often collect vast quantities of data and, in some cases, have specialist librarians assigned solely to collecting and manipulating information that is in quantitative form.

The statistical tables and reports routinely released by the U.S. Census Bureau are especially good sources with freely available data. This is discussed in the last section of this chapter. There are also other leading tools for locating quantitative data. *Lexis Nexis Statistical* is a well known commercial database product that indexes large volumes of statistical reports generated by the U.S. federal government, international agencies, state and local governments, businesses, and not for profit organizations. Newspapers and general interest magazines will from time to time also report sets of quantitative data pertinent to your topic. Quantitative data can be found in academic books and journal articles and within specialized trade publications like business journals or magazines that target readers in a profession, such as law enforcement officers, educators, or social workers.

Valuable quantitative data is frequently available online but often only through what many have referred to as the "invisible Web." This means that the actual numbers pertinent to your topic of interest may not be retrieved at all if you enter a typical Google search for that information. On the contrary, the detailed reporting of that quantitative data is often "invisible" to search engines like Google or Yahoo because it is contained deep within government or private websites, inside reports that do not pop up in reply to general searches on the Internet. A far better technique for locating this quantitative data online is to use what you learn during your general searches of articles, newspapers, and the Internet to identify the specific proper names of government agencies or public and private organizations connected to your topic (e.g., "The Bureau of Labor Statistics" for a topic relating to jobs or the "Small Business Administration" for a topic that deals with small private companies). Next, visit the websites for those agencies and organizations and look for links on those sites with titles such as "research," "data," "publications," "policy briefs," "working papers," "reports," or "library."

Whenever coming upon a statistical table, graph, or chart of numbers in a book, article, or website, scan down to see if the name of a private organization or government agency is listed as a source. You can then visit the website for that named organization, which frequently unlocks a wealth of related statistical data. Likewise, if the name of a specific statistical report is mentioned (e.g., *Uniform Crime Reports* or *Digest of Education Statistics*, etc.), you can also try searching that online or in the online catalog of your public or college library.

Last but not least, for those with access to the *Proquest Research Library* commercial database, one of the helpful "advanced" search options they provide is the ability to limit results to a document type called "statistics." This will filter out articles that do not contain at least some numeric data relating to the other subject words you enter as part of your search.

Newspaper Articles

Newspapers are powerful sources of information on both societal problems and public policy ideas. Their advantage is that they provide current information. One weakness is that they only provide the latest information, making it more difficult to understand the background on a policy topic.

Two major newspapers at the national level are *The New York Times* and *USA-Today*. Coverage of state and local policies requires that you look at more regional newspapers. Fortunately, many newspapers can be accessed on the Internet. *The New York Times* and *USA-Today* have free daily updates, and many local newspapers have similar access. Be aware that reviewing the older issues of these papers online will usually not be free, and this is where a visit to a public or academic library or to an online subscription database may be required.

A valuable commercial database for newspaper searching is the *Proquest Research Library*. Other leading commercial databases providing newspaper access include *Lexis Nexis* and *Gale Custom Newspapers*.

The study of public policy requires current information because ultimately its purpose is to come up with policy decisions that will improve current societal conditions. For that reason, develop your skills in finding information within sources that are up to date, and that means newspapers and magazines, sometimes called "journals" when they are academic.

Magazines and Journals

For public policy issues, valuable sources of information are found in magazine and journal articles, all of which are referred to as periodical literature.

Magazine and journal articles can be used to provide both background information and current developments in your public policy issue. Magazines tend to contain more general information and rarely offer articles that cite their underlying sources in a formal manner; journal articles rely more heavily upon research and usually provide formal lists of outside sources.

Because many articles are published every year, you need some tool to help you locate those articles that are appropriate to your topic. You can locate appropriate articles by using abstracting and indexing tools more commonly referred to as online "databases." In many cases, the full text of these periodical articles may be available for reading online, sometimes presented in both HTML and PDF formats. PDFs offer an exact image of the written source as if one held the original print version in one's hand, including images of any and all charts, graphs, tables, drawings, cartoons, or color photographs appearing in that article source.

There are two kinds of databases you should consider when looking for magazine and journal articles:

1. General Databases: These cover a large number of periodicals on a variety of subjects.

2. Subject Specific Databases: These cover a large number of periodicals on a particular subject such as education, social policy, or crime.

A comprehensive database source as of the time this book was published is *Proquest Research Library*, which is a commercial database often available through your college, high school, or community library. Some private companies also may subscribe. Here is a short list of additional commercial databases you may find helpful. There are hundreds of possibilities, but these are some of the more widely known:

General Databases:

- *Expanded Academic ASAP.* Thomson Gale.

  Covers a variety of current subjects via popular magazines, as well as scholarly journals, often available in full-text online. Provides excellent indexing of articles by subject terms.

- *MasterFile Select.* EBSCO Publishing.

  A collection of hundreds of popular magazines covering business, science, health, the humanities, and other subjects.

- *Readers Guide Abstracts.* H.W. Wilson.

  Database version of the well-known *Readers Guide to Periodical Literature*, frequently found in both public and college libraries. Indexes most popular U.S. general interest magazines.

- *WilsonSelectPlus.* H.W. Wilson.

Another commonly used general index of popular magazines, academic journals, and business publications. Links that provide the full-text of these articles are often available.

Subject Specific Databases:

The databases listed below may be helpful to you on specific topics.

■ *ABI Inform.* Proquest.

A leading collection of articles from well known journals in business and management. Most available in full online.

■ *AgeLine.* American Association of Retired Persons.

Indexes literature relevant to social gerontology and the health, social, and economic contexts of aging.

■ *Communication and Mass Media Index.* EBSCO.

Covers over 600 journal titles pertinent to communications and mass media.

■ *Criminal Justice Abstracts.* Sage.

Indexes books, journals, and other reports pertinent to crime and criminal justice topics.

■ *Education Abstracts.* H.W. Wilson.

Covers a wide variety of popular, professional, and academic publications touching on all aspects within the field of education.

■ *GenderWatch.* Proquest.

A specialized index of magazines, books, academic journal articles, and more covering topics pertinent to gender roles and relationships, including public policy aspects of gender.

■ *PAIS.* Public Affairs Information Service.

Provides indexing and abstracting of articles, books, conference proceedings, government documents, book chapters, and statistical directories about public affairs.

■ *Race Relations Abstracts.* Sage.

Covers books, academic journal articles, and conference papers in the area of race relations. Issues covered include discrimination, education, employment, health, politics, law, and legislation.

■ *Social Work Abstracts.* National Association of Social Workers.

Indexes journals that address social work and closely related topics such as homelessness, AIDS, child and family welfare, aging, substance abuse, and more.

- *Sociological Abstracts.* Cambridge Scientific Abstracts.

Provides indexing and abstracting of journals, book chapters, conference papers, and other sources in sociology and related fields such as the sociology of crime, health and medicine, political sociology, sociology of sports, and more.

Books

Although much of the information required for research can be found in journals and newspapers, you often need in-depth, detailed information which can only be found in books. Information in books is not as current as what you can find in newspapers, magazines, and journal articles. By becoming familiar with the system of organization in your library, the job of locating books becomes much easier. Books are found on shelves by their call numbers.

Most libraries use one of two major classification systems for organizing their collection: the Library of Congress System or the Dewey Decimal System. Under both of these systems, the call numbers arrange materials according to similar subjects. A different call number is assigned to each item in the library. Under the Library of Congress System, the books are coded by a combination of letters and numbers, beginning with a letter or letters.

Searching your library's online catalog will help you identify the call numbers of the items you wish to locate. A good technique for finding materials on a particular topic in an online catalog is to do a keyword search or, alternatively, a more precisely entered subject search.

Usually a subject search means that you choose words from a controlled (i.e., established) vocabulary. In colleges and universities throughout the United States, the controlled vocabulary most often used is the *Library of Congress Subject Headings.* A keyword search means you use whatever words you think describe your topic. You can then review the citations retrieved, look at the subject headings used in records most relevant to your topic, and refine your searching by doing specific subject searches.

Here are some final pieces of advice for searching online catalogs in order to locate books about your topic:

- Incorporate Library of Congress Subject Headings into your online catalog searching process.

- Do not be too inflexible when entering keywords into a library's online catalog. Practice healthy doses of trial and error by entering combinations of different single words or short phrases potentially related to your topic.

- Shy away from entering obscure phrases that are too lengthy. When you do enter a phrase(s), enclose it in quotation marks (e.g., "No Child Left Behind").

- Use the catalog's "advanced" search screens when entering more than a single word or phrase.

- Become comfortable with narrowing and broadening your catalog searches. Try entering fewer search terms if you got a very short list of results; or, on the contrary, add additional, narrowing terms if a list of results is too long or filled with irrelevant titles.

- Recognize that words in catalog and database records can be singular or plural. Consider using "truncation" searching, which involves entering a symbol, often an asterisk, following the root of a word. Thus, a search for "parent*" retrieves all book records that refer to the terms "parent," "parents," "parental," "parenting," etc.

- Be aware that not all topics have dozens of recent books written about them, especially narrow or geographically specialized subjects (e.g., "economic development in upstate New York"). You are more likely to find that discussion inside articles or government publications, not books.

United States Government Publications

Every year, the United States government publishes hundreds of thousands of pages of material on thousands of different subjects. These materials can be very valuable in studying both societal problems and existing and proposed public policies. In the last decade, much of the material has been digitized so that you can access it through websites. Older material may not be found this way, in which case you will have to use items that may be available in print (paper) and microfiche from a library.

Here are some basic websites you can use to locate government publications:

> *Firstgov* **http://www.firstgov.gov** :
> The U.S. government's official Web portal. One can look up information according to a broad list of public policy topics, different levels of government (e.g., federal, state, local) or an A to Z list of specific government agencies.

> *GPO* **http://www.gpoaccess.gov/** :
> Official website of the United States Government Printing Office. It includes a link to a searchable "Catalog of U.S. Government Publications." This site is also browseable according to publications coming from the

three branches of the U.S. federal government (e.g., browse Congressional bills, the Congressional Record, the Federal Register, U.S. Presidential materials, and information on U.S. Supreme Court opinions).

Thomas **http://thomas.loc.gov/** :
Thomas is a primary online source for information about legislative actions and publications for both houses of the U.S. Congress.

Stateline **http://www.stateline.org/** :
Funded by the Pew Research Center and Pew Charitable Trusts, this weekly online compilation of state level public policy information is aimed at journalists, students, law makers, and ordinary citizens.

National Conference of State Legislatures **http://www.ncsl.org/** :
The site includes an A to Z list covering state and federal public policy issues as well as links to the specific legislative bodies within all of the fifty U.S. states.

Cities Online
http://www.usmayors.org/uscm/meet_mayors/cities_online/ :
This is a project of the U.S. Conference of Mayors and links to websites for city and town governments all across the U.S.

Online library catalogs can be helpful for accessing government publications. Some academic and public libraries participate in "depository" relationships with the government, whereby they collect and catalog large percentages of these publications. The U.S. Government Printing Office provides an online list of federal depository libraries at: http://www.gpoaccess.gov/libraries.html

In addition, a variety of commercial databases include government sources, such as Proquest's SIRS Government Reporter.

Non-Governmental Policy Publications

Over the past four decades, hundreds of organizations have emerged that conduct and publish information about public policy questions. Some organizations cover a broad range of domestic and foreign topics. These include the Brookings Institution and the American Enterprise Institute. Others are focused on a specific policy area like the Urban Institute or the Children's Defense Fund. Some have a broad membership base like the American Association of Retired People (AARP) and some, like Brookings, have a small governing board. Some offer websites that analyze current public policy issues, such as PublicAgenda.org.

All of these organizations have some kind of ideological position, but some are more careful than others in presenting both sides and following the standards of good scholarship. As a public policy analyst, you should be aware of their orientation in using their information.

A good general approach to finding non-governmental policy publications is to use the *CQ Researcher*. Many schools and colleges subscribe. The *"CQ"* stands for *Congressional Quarterly*, but it is not a government publication. Over the years, this company has become a respected source of information about public policy. Their reports on a wide array of topics include extensive bibliographies along with links to important contact organizations connected to coverage of all sides of various public policy matters.

United States Census Data

The official counting of a nation's people and businesses is a practice that has been done for centuries. The first U.S. Census took place in1790. In the United States of the twenty-first century, a wide variety of special types of government documents are published by the United States Bureau of the Census. Every ten years, the Bureau collects information on population and housing for the entire country. Additional detailed quantitative information is collected as to social, economic, and other demographic characteristics that involve far more than simply counting heads. Detailed data reports address various aspects of jobs, incomes, the national economy, and educational achievement, as well as various lifestyle issues, even how long people in the U.S. typically spend traveling to work in a given region and how they accomplish that (i.e., driving vs. walking vs. public transportation, etc.). This information is updated within the ten-year period itself through estimates and other sample surveys.

Learn to use the U.S. Census website well, because it will be of great use in many settings. At that site, http://www.census.gov, one can also find an explanation of how the most recent decennial census took place, by visiting the publication entitled *Census 2000 Basics*. This was issued by the Bureau in September of 2002. The Census Bureau website is one where you can easily get lost inside numerous statistical reports and complex data tables. However, two specific data mining tools on that site are particularly worth pointing out. These are:

> *American FactFinder:* A quick way to access a variety of commonly sought after Census information for a state, county, city, or zip code of interest. Use this tool to locate that area's total population, racial composition, per capita income, percentage of individuals living below the poverty line, percentage who graduated from high school, and more.

Population Finder: This is accessed using a link inside of the "American FactFinder." It is a tool that allows you to enter a specific state, county, city, or zip code and provides you with a quick snapshot of the population trends for that area over the past 10 to 15 years. It also allows you to retrieve lists of population for a state or county, ranked according to total population, or listed alphabetically. This is useful when you want to determine other areas in the country, or other areas in one's own state, that are of comparable population size.

A final resource that should be mentioned when you are seeking statistical data compiled by the U.S. Census Bureau is the well known reference, *Statistical Abstract of the United States.* Most libraries have the print edition of this within their reference collections, and it is also freely available on the Internet. Published by the Bureau, it is a handy guide to a wide array of statistical tables originating within numerous U.S. governmental agencies. It may not always go into detail regarding all aspects of your topic, but for most public policy matters, it offers pertinent quantitative data that is recent, along with historical trends.

Profile of an Expert User of Information

Robert Watson

Robert Watson is a very successful corporate leader in the healthcare field. His specialty is taking over companies for investors and making them profitable. After graduating from the Syracuse University Policy Studies program in 1979, he received his MBA from the Wharton School at the University of Pennsylvania. One of the keys to his success is finding the information he needs to make the right decision. Watson also encourages his companies to give time and money to local charities. One of his companies cleaned, painted, and restocked the Ronald McDonald House at the Children's Hospital of Oakland California.

Chapter 3

Gathering Information from Players and Experts

"It is the province of knowledge to speak, and it is the privilege of wisdom to listen."

— Oliver Wendell Holmes

YOUR GOAL   To develop skills in locating and interviewing players and experts.

Introduction

Published information about public policies needs to be supplemented by information obtained from people who have varying degrees of knowledge and experience with the policy topic. This chapter will help you figure out what people you need to gather information from and how you will do it. There are three general categories of such people:

- Players, which include government officials and their staff who make or administer laws, and individuals and members of interest groups who work to influence the public policy-making process

- Experts who attempt to provide a knowledgeable viewpoint to help players and stakeholders

- Stakeholders who are impacted by the policy but do not have power or expertise

Players and experts are usually contacted personally through phone, e-mail, or in person and are interviewed. Stakeholders may be interviewed individually, but to assess their opinions as a group, they should be surveyed in a systematic way. The next chapter will describe the ways to go about surveying stakeholders. This chapter will describe what kinds of information are available from players and experts, how to locate key people to interview, and how to obtain the most detailed and accurate information possible.

Individual Interviews

Interviewing players and experts is essential for good public policy analysis. These individuals are likely to have an up-to-date grasp of the information and get you on your way to asking the right questions of written information and others you might interview. However, just like the print information, you have to be careful to select knowledgeable players and experts and to understand what biases they may have.

In Chapter 2, we pointed out how to get started in searching for published information. If you know nothing, you will not know what information to look for, but if you do not have any information, you will know nothing. The only strategy to follow is to acquire a little information at the time in order to figure out what more information you need.

Not only is this advice true for gathering information from published sources; it is also true in gathering information from experts and players in your policy field. If you know nothing about a topic like crime, you would not want to call up the District Attorney and say something like, "tell me all you know about crime." If you tried that, you would not get useful information, and the DA would tell you to do your homework before talking to her. You would want to study the topic and perhaps find a current area, such as drunk driving, that the DA has been working on. You could then ask her what her policy idea is or what she knows is going on in other counties. When the DA sees you have done your homework, she will give you much more information.

Players and experts are more likely to help you if they are convinced that you are actively involved in the subject. For that reason, before directly contacting a knowledgeable individual, develop a basic knowledge of the subject and formulate a clear idea of the information you want to obtain.

What to Ask

In deciding what specific information you want to obtain, consider the following example. Suppose that you are interested in your school district's policy on closing school for bad weather. Here are some questions to ask: Who makes the final decision? Are there guidelines from the state about the factors that should be considered? How does the person making the decision get information about the weather conditions? Formulate questions you might ask with respect to the following:

Public policy: What relevant laws exist or are proposed? Which administrative agencies are responsible for implementing the laws? Have any courts made relevant judicial decisions? What has been the impact of the laws? What new laws are now being considered?

Societal problems: What are they? What studies exist about these problems? What studies are planned? How different will they be in the future?

Players: What are the key individuals, groups, and institutions responsible for the policy? Do they support or oppose the current policy? How much power do they have? How important is the issue to them?

Evidence: What evidence shows that the societal problem exists?

Policy alternative: Is there an alternative policy that could work to ameliorate the societal problem?

Before writing an e-mail or conducting a face-to-face interview, make a list of your goals. What do you expect to gain from contacting this person? This will make writing the e-mail easier. Also, formulate questions ahead of time and write them down. Questions can be as specific as you wish, depending on the individual.

Some examples of basic questions that can be asked of any player are:

- What evidence is available about your problem?

- What policies exist that deal with your problem? How well do they work? Who is in charge of them?

- What studies have been done on your problem?

- Who are the key players and what are their positions? How much power do they have? How important is this issue to them?

- What public polices have been proposed to deal with your societal problem?

Before sending an e-mail, read it carefully for typographical, grammatical, and spelling errors. Also, make sure the e-mail is neat. Always answer e-mails or requests for information promptly.

Locating Players and Experts

Once you have acquired basic background information about your public policy issue and you have developed questions to ask, select the people you want to contact for more information. You should think carefully about who you will contact. First, consider who will be making the policy decision and who will be influencing the decision makers. For example, your investigation of school policy on the cancellation of classes for bad weather might lead you to the decision maker, the District Superintendent. Players who would influence the Superintendent might include an officer of the parent-teacher organization, so you could contact a PTA officer.

In deciding on which players and experts you wish to contact, balance how easy it will be to contact the person with how much information the person is likely to give you. Generally, the people with the best information are the most difficult to contact. You may want to begin with someone you can easily contact and ask for suggestions and even an introduction to someone more knowledgeable.

From your background research, select the names of people and organizations that are mentioned in the news, books, and articles and in websites. You may also try to contact experts, such as researchers at universities and think tanks who have published on the subject.

The telephone book is an essential tool for locating knowledgeable people, even if you do not have a specific name of an individual or organization. Telephone numbers of local, state, and federal government offices appear in the telephone book in a separate section called "The Blue Pages." Non-government agencies are listed in the yellow pages under such headings as *social service organizations,* *"environmental conservation and ecological organizations," "drug abuse and addiction information and treatment," and "business and trade organizations."* Formal pressure groups may be listed in the yellow pages by subject or in the general (white pages) section by name.

If you have located the organization in the telephone book but do not know the name of a specific individual who can answer your questions, take the following steps: (1) call the main number, (2) identify yourself, (3) state the purpose of your call, and (4) ask for the name of someone who can provide information on your topic.

Next to the telephone, the web is the best source for tracking down players and experts. You can try a general Google search by putting in the subject, but that may only generate long lists of irrelevant people. It would be better to use the websites of government and non-profit organizations. The research skills developed in

Chapter 2 will help you track down players and experts. You can start with the websites of your county executive, state senator, or other elected state or local officials. You can also visit the League of Women Voters website at www.lwv.org for lists of government officials.

Once you have decided on the people and organizations you wish to contact, decide whether you will use the telephone, make a personal visit, write a letter, or send an e-mail. Initially, the telephone is the best way to make sure that the person is willing and able to provide the information. Obtaining the information at the time of the initial telephone call would be most efficient. However, the interviewee may prefer a written request or a personal visit. The written request may be part of the organization's procedure. A personal visit, if possible, is always useful because you may be introduced to other people to interview, and you may be able to study or even acquire written material. Always ask the people you interview to suggest others to be contacted. In addition, ask for written material that they have on a website or that can be sent to you through e-mail or the mail.

Watching Out for Bias

Obtaining detailed and accurate information from a knowledgeable person requires you to be as informed as possible. We have already emphasized that you should have background information on the public policy issues in order to select the person you want to contact in the first place. Once you contact that person, the more specific the questions, the better.

Various types of people may give you biased information. Government officials will almost always provide you with the official viewpoint and will try to avoid controversy. As a result, the information will tend to be vague. People who are trying to influence government policy will explain things in ways that support their positions and self-interest. Journalists and academic researchers will claim they are objective, but they may also have a particular orientation. Also, the person you are talking to may not know the information but may guess at it.

The best way to guard against possible bias is to ask the same question of two or more people that you know have different views on the public policy issue. If people on different sides of an issue give you the same information, you can have some confidence that the information is accurate. If you receive conflicting information, you may have to interview additional people, check other sources, or at least take into account the questionable nature of the information as you analyze your topic. This advice is the same in dealing with written information. The only ways to protect against biased and limited information are to obtain the information from multiple sources and to carefully check for inconsistencies.

Planning a Strategy to Contact Players and Experts

It takes time to obtain information from people and organizations. Therefore, develop a plan that will be completed over several weeks or even months. The plan might include the following:

1. Compile a list of knowledgeable experts and players that are concerned with your societal problem. Include people from universities, the business community, the government, and non-profit organizations. Obtain the address and telephone number of each person on the list. This may require initial telephone calls to make sure you have the correct address and name. This will take one to two weeks.

2. Send an e-mail as soon as you identify each person.

3. Call each person after you have sent the e-mails. Be prepared to ask some of your questions at this time, as well as to schedule a face-to-face meeting. Ask for material to be sent to you.

4. After your final contact, send a thank you note or an email indicating how your study is progressing.

5. Be prepared to make several contacts with those who provide you with the most useful information. The most important goal would be for them to agree to react to your written ideas. Make a personal visit if possible.

Adjust these actions as a result of the responses you receive. Most people you contact will be interested but busy, so do everything you can to minimize the time and effort required for them to help you. Be accommodating with schedules and offer gratitude at every turn.

Profile of a Policy Butterfly

Felicia Feinerman

Felicia Feinerman grew up in Queens, New York, which, like the rest of the Big Apple, faces the problems of many big cities. She has first-rate communication skills and knows how to make friends, and therefore, how to get information from everyone. As one of my students, she was a great undergraduate teaching assistant and an office worker. When she participated in the NYS Assembly Internship Program in her junior year, the Assemblyman she worked for offered her a position as his Legislative Director, which she took after completing her degree. Her ability to tap players and experts for technical information made her a valuable legislative aide to the Assemblyman on important legislation. When he left Albany to become the Manhattan Borough President, he took Felicia with him. Whenever I need detailed and correct information about state legislation, I call Felicia.

Chapter 4

Surveying Stakeholders

"If one or two people tell you that you're an ass, you can ignore them. But if three or four people tell you you're an ass, you might think about putting on a saddle."

— Yiddish saying

YOUR GOAL   To define the purpose, select the sample, write the questions, plan the method of contact, and estimate the costs for a survey.

Introduction

Surveys are like personal interviews, except they are designed to get information from a large number of people. In public policy analysis, most surveys are used to determine the views of those impacted by the policy. As already noted, we call these people "stakeholders." A large number of players or experts can also be surveyed but as a beginning public policy analyst, you are not likely to be doing that kind of research. This chapter introduces you to the basic principles of survey design for large groups of people. For additional information about surveys, you should refer to Chapter 15: Guide to Conducting Sample Surveys.

To understand surveys, you must master these concepts:

- **Factual Information**: What people perceive to be true or fact.

- **Attitudinal Information**: How people feel (positive or negative) about societal problems or public policies.

- **Target Population**: The entire group of individuals about whom you want to gather information.

- **Sample**: Those individuals chosen from the total target population from whom you gather information.

- **Sampling Frame**: The total number of individuals that you contact for your survey.

- **Sample Size**: The actual number of responses you receive.

- **Confidence Interval**: An estimate of how close the findings generated by the sample would be to the findings if everyone in the target population were surveyed.

- **Random Sampling**: All subjects have an equal chance of being selected.

- **Non-random Sampling (Convenience Sampling)**: Subjects are not selected by chance.

- **Simple Random Sampling**: Randomly selecting respondents from a complete list of the target population.

- **Cluster Sampling**: Acquire a complete list of locations where your target population can be found, randomly select locations from the list, and contact enough individuals at each location to fulfill your goals for a sample.

- **Sampling Bias**: Occurs when a category of the target population is over- or underrepresented in the sample.

- **Response Rate**: The percentage of the sample that responds when contacted for a survey.

- **Closed-Choice Question**: Limits the kinds of answers the respondent may give, requiring a choice of one or more of the answers provided by the question.

- **Open-Ended Question**: Allows subjects to answer the questions without restrictions imposed by the wording.

Determine What Your Client Wants

The purpose of this chapter is to gather survey information as though you were hired by a client. A client is any player trying to make a decision. You might conduct a survey for a government official who wants to assess the impact of a policy, for a non-profit agency that seeks more information on its clients, or for a pressure group hoping to use the results to support its views. By considering for whom the information is to be gathered and for what purpose they hope to use it, you will have a clearer picture of what questions to ask and what people you will need to approach for answers. For example, an Assistant Superintendent of Schools may want a survey conducted on students who drop out of high school in the local school district. Others in addition to your client, such as the school board, the parent-teacher organization, students, and other players might also use the data you collect.

Players and experts who study and make public policy need to know how the people impacted by policies are affected by them. They want to know the degree to which these people are "causing" the problem as well as how the problem shapes what they do in their daily lives. Just as market researchers do surveys to find out how potential customers will react to a new product or value existing products, public policy researchers do surveys to determine what the consequences of existing and proposed policies might be. For that reason, when you plan a survey, consider first who will be using the information you gather and for what purpose they want the information.

Although your purpose is to gather accurate information for your client, the way questions are posed, as well as other research decisions, may introduce biases. The key test is the degree to which the procedures used to collect the information are a reasonable approach to acquiring accurate information.

Conduct surveys only for clients willing to allow you to follow proper procedures. The proper purpose of a survey is not to prove a point but to gather and report information that will help players make good decisions. For example, a survey should not be conducted to prove that all people feel the seat belt law deprives them of their liberty; rather, a survey could be conducted to discover what people are saying about their unwillingness to obey the seat belt law in order to see if new laws are needed. A survey never tells you whether a policy is good or bad or whether it should or should not be implemented. It only gives you information on conditions, people's attitudes, behavior, or perceptions of facts that players can use as one factor in deciding how to deal with societal problems.

You may obtain factual and attitudinal information with surveys. **Factual information** consists of such things as the occupations of a particular group of people, their incomes, their reported behavior, their physical environment, or their use of various government services. For example, a study of mandatory seat belt use in New York State might ask people whether or not they personally use seat belts. The information derived from such a question would indicate how many people say they use seat belts.

Attitudinal information indicates how people feel about societal problems or about public policies designed to deal with those problems. In the mandatory seat belt example, a survey might determine if people feel more secure when they wear seat belts. In order to design and implement a useful survey, determine whether you are seeking attitudinal or factual responses for each question you design. The term "feel" is used to mean whether the respondent likes or dislikes or has a positive or negative attitude to a societal condition or a policy.

Pay close attention to the fit between the client's goals and the information your survey will provide. The best first step is to ask what the client wants to find out and then to make sure that it is compatible with the client's goals. Sometimes, you may need to ask the client to more clearly state the goals and then check to see if the questions are compatible.

A key element in determining the client's purpose is to clearly identify the target population. The **target population** is the entire group of individuals about whom you want to gather information. Make sure that your client agrees about the group of people whose views are sought. Without this, the client's purpose is unclear and the survey will be useless.

A target population must be carefully defined in ways that are appropriate to the particular questions you are examining. The most well-known types of surveys are public opinion polls of the entire adult population in the United States, such as a survey to find out the preferences of the public for candidates in an upcoming election. However, smaller sample surveys of specialized target populations are usually more valuable for policy analysis because key groups of people may be more knowledgeable about policy, are more directly affected by a particular policy, or are in a better position to influence policy. For example, in a survey of the uses of food stamps, a sample drawn from the users of food stamps would be more appropriate than a sample drawn from the general population.

Defining a target population appropriate to your purpose involves determining its approximate size and geographical scope. For example, your target population could be the 12,000 doctors who work in a local community. Unless you are specific about the size and location as well as who is included, you cannot design a useful survey. When defining the target population, make sure that the reader of your final report will be able to determine who is and who is not in the target population.

Choosing a Sample Population

The **sample** consists of those individuals chosen from the total target population from which you gather information. In seeking a sample, you have to make decisions about two questions, "How big should the sample be?" and "What procedures should be used to select the individuals in the sample?" Since, in most cases, it is impossible to survey everyone in the target population, you will want to generalize the responses obtained from your sample to the entire target population. Therefore, you must attempt to select as your sample a group of individuals that is representative of the target population. The goal of sampling is to select a group of subjects whose responses would be as similar as possible to the responses if everyone in the target population responded to the survey.

The term **sample size** refers to the actual number of responses to your survey you receive, not the total number of individuals that you contact from some list or other source of potential respondents, called the **sampling frame**. As we shall discuss below, in some procedures, the response rate may be very low, requiring you to contact a large number of potential respondents in order to obtain a sample of adequate size. This section gives you some general guidelines on determining what your sample size should be.

The size of a sample is primarily determined by the resources you have available, the kind of analysis you will be undertaking, and the desired accuracy. To a much smaller degree, the size of the target population should also be taken into account. In general, the larger the sample, the better. However, obtaining a large sample is very costly in terms of time and money, so carefully calculate how large a sample you will need. Work to obtain a sample of the requisite size, but do not gather a sample larger than you can afford.

In deciding on sample size, consider what analysis of subgroups of the sample you will be carrying out. In a study of the use of food stamps in a particular county, for example, your sample of food stamp users might be analyzed according to the distribution of such important features as age, gender, and income level. The characteristics of the population may be extremely important in some cases. For example, surveys may show differences between females and males on questions pertaining to abortion rights and similar topics. Racial and ethnic differences tend to be strongly associated with opinions on racial equality.

These considerations should shape your decision on the size of the sample. For example, you may obtain a sample of 500, which is an adequate sample for most purposes. But you may be interested in comparing different subgroups of that sample, such as categories defined by age, occupation, sex, or other important features. In such a situation, you will wind up analyzing subgroups much smaller than the total of 500 and the confidence interval (see pp. 42–43) will be accordingly much wider. If you identify five occupational groups, for example, each such group might average only 100, and some groups may be much smaller if the sample is not equally distributed among the occupational groups. The more subgroups that you want to analyze, the bigger the sample should be.

The most important aspect of a sample is its absolute size: 100, 500, 1,000, or whatever. The number in the sample is much more important than what proportion of the total population this number represents. This principle of sample selection is sometimes difficult to grasp by novice survey researchers. Nevertheless, the fact that a sample consists of 500 individuals, for example, is more important than whether the number 500 represents .1 percent, 1 percent, 10 percent, or some other percentage of the target population. (This assumes that the sample was randomly selected.) Accurate samples of the total United States population can consist of fewer than 1,500 people. A sample of this size represents only about .00001 of the total population, but when correctly selected, it can usually give an accurate representation of the entire population.

The size of the sample is most important because it determines what is called the **confidence interval**. The idea behind a confidence interval is that it gives you an estimate of how close the findings generated by the sample would be to the findings if everyone in the target population were surveyed. The confidence interval procedure can be used only with samples that are selected randomly. (See the next section on sample selection.) The confidence interval tells you the likely difference between the results of your sample and the actual situation in the entire target population.

In general, the larger the absolute size of the sample, the smaller the range above or below a reported number the confidence interval will be. We generally use a 95 percent confidence interval. For example, if you obtained an approval rating of 58% from a sample of 100 respondents, the confidence interval would be +/-10%. In other words, in 95% of the cases of a hypothetical repeated survey sampling, the approval rating would be in the range of 48%-68% (58%+/-10%). If you obtained the same 58% from a sample of 350, the 95% confidence interval would be +/-5%, or 53%-63%, a much smaller range within which you could be confident that the results would fall 95% of the time.

Figure 4.1 displays the minimum 95 percent confidence interval for a given sample size; that is, the confidence interval when the random sample is a small percentage of the target population. When a sample represents nearly all the target population, its 95 percent confidence interval number is smaller. Books covering survey research contain more complex tables that provide confidence intervals for graphs that represent a large percentage of a population. Figure 4.1 is a conservative estimate useful for most purposes.

Figure 4.1: 95% Confidence Interval
(For Simple Random Samples Only)

Sample Size	There is a 95% chance that the figure in the target population will be within the following percentage (either plus or minus) of the figure in the sample.
30	18%
35	17%
40	15%
50	14%
60	13%
70	12%
80	11%
90	10%
100	10%
120	9%
140	8%
160	8%
180	7%
200	7%
250	6%
300	6%
350	5%
400	5%
600	4%
700	4%
800	3%
900	3%
1000	3%
1500	3%
2500	2%

Source: Calculated from O' Sullivan, E., and Russell, G. (1994). *Research methods for public administrators*. White Plains, NY: Longman.

Using this table, you can choose your sample size by deciding how big the range of your results you are willing to accept. A sample of over 1,500 will give you the small range of +/-3%, while a sample of 100 will give you a range of +/-10%. If you are unable to obtain a sample that is large enough to give you a small range, you should still report the findings to your client and recommend to your client that a larger sample should be taken. Most people find confidence intervals above +/-5% to limit the scope of the findings substantially.

Sample Selection

Samples can be selected using either **random** or **non-random** methods. In survey research, the word random refers to a specific procedure in which all subjects have an equal chance of being selected. In this case, random does not mean haphazard or arbitrary, as it frequently does in ordinary conversation.

By contrast, in **non-random sampling**, subjects are not selected by chance. Non-random sampling is also called **convenience sampling**. Examples include contacting shoppers at a shopping center or calling the first 100 people on a phone list. Surveys based on non-random sampling cannot be generalized reliably beyond the people actually surveyed.

A sampling procedure must be evaluated by its ability to satisfy the objectives of the survey given the amount of time and money available. Although random sampling is preferred in every case, time and respondent availability sometimes make it very difficult. Two of the most frequently used random sampling methods are called **simple random sampling** and **cluster sampling**.

In order to employ simple random sampling, you need access to a complete list of everyone in a target population, and you must have equal access to all members of the population. Using such a list, you can begin at a randomly selected point and select a sample from the list, skipping enough names as you proceed through the list to pick the names you will attempt to contact. For example, you may start with the sixth name on the list and choose every 20th name thereafter. A more widely accepted procedure among professional survey researchers is to use a random number table, which is a list of numbers generated by a computer that has no pattern.

If you are planning to select a sample from a target population of a particular group, you will probably be able to obtain a membership list from which you can randomly select respondents. Telephone numbers and addresses are usually available from such lists, but be aware that the lists may contain inaccuracies. The older the list and the less organized the group, the more inaccurate the list. In some cases, a client may want you to generate a target population from several lists. For example, a social service agency may ask you to obtain the membership lists of all churches in a specific area. The combination of these lists would then constitute the target population, although each list may vary in quality.

If you are planning to draw a sample from the general population, no comprehensive list of all members exists. A telephone directory comes close to such a list, since about 90 percent of all homes contain telephones. However, those people who lack telephones, such as the low-income, the elderly, and rural residents, may introduce biases in a sample that is drawn from the telephone directory. In addition, many people maintain unlisted telephone numbers, have two or more numbers, or more recently, use a cell phone exclusively and do not have a land line. Depending on the purposes of your survey, such under-representation may or may not represent a problem. If it is a problem, a variety of techniques can be used to compensate for such sampling problems, as discussed below.

An alternative source listing of households for many medium-sized cities is a series of publications called the *Polk Directories,* published by R.L. Polk and Company of New York, which may be available in your local library. These directories list the names, telephone numbers, and addresses of city residents, so they can be used for face-to-face, telephone, or mail contacts. There are also CD-ROMS of phone numbers available that can be used.

In the absence (or unavailability) of a complete list of everyone in your target population, you cannot employ simple random sampling, but you can still use a method that is almost as good and is widely used by professional survey researchers. This is the procedure called **cluster sampling**.

To use cluster sampling, first identify a series of locations where your target population may be found (such as classrooms, residence halls, or areas of a city). Obtain (or create) a complete list of such locations, and randomly select locations from this list. At each location selected, contact enough individuals to fulfill your goals for a sample.

These procedures are used in choosing national samples of the American population: randomly selecting states, counties, and regions within counties. It can be used in any situation in which you can develop a method for selecting individuals from a randomly chosen location.

Sampling Bias

No matter what sampling procedure you use, be sensitive about over-sampling or under-sampling certain categories of respondents, unless you have some reason for over-sampling certain key subgroups. For example, a list of all the doctors in a certain region may not be completely up to date and thus will underreport younger doctors and those who have recently moved into the area. As previously mentioned, sampling from the telephone book will result in some bias. It will bypass any individuals who do not own a telephone or who have some unlisted telephone numbers.

To check for **sampling bias**, compare key characteristics of the respondents in your sample to those in your target population. Your goal is to achieve the same percentages in your sample as in your target population. A perfect match is almost never achieved. But, at minimum, you should report how close or divergent your sample and target populations are with respect to key characteristics. Beyond this, you can report the significance of any difference, and take some actions to reduce problems caused by any significant differences. Figure 16.9, Chapter 16, page 200 gives you the basis for evaluating the difference between your sample and the population.

For example, if you know that the male-female ratio in your target population is 50-50, a sample with 45 percent males (a 5 percentage point difference) is not significantly discrepant unless the population is at least 1,500 and the sample is at least 600. However, a sample containing 30 percent males (a 20 percentage point difference) is significantly discrepant for populations as small as 150 and samples as small as 90. Larger populations or samples will result in dubious results because of such a wide divergence.

Be sure that any biases found in your sample will not seriously affect the results of your survey. For example, if you feel that your procedures are biased in some way, such as by omitting people with unlisted phone numbers, that your sample will seriously misrepresent your target population, you may undertake any of the following steps: (1) supplement with a door-to-door survey, and (2) acknowledge the bias in your report and specify how this bias may affect your results. Even those with unlisted telephone numbers can be contacted by randomly dialing the last four digits of a telephone number. Of course, this procedure results in dialing many non-working numbers.

The kinds of variables that you will want to compare depend on the purpose of your survey and also on the statistics you can obtain for your target population. Sex, age, race, and geographic locations are the variables most frequently used. For example, suppose you were studying a sample of undergraduate college students chosen from a target population of all undergraduates. If the topic had to do with the rules on who registered for classes first, class standing would be an important characteristic. In such a case it would be a good idea to present the class standing

Figure 4.2: Comparison of Target Population and Sample of Undergraduates, Citrus University, Fall Semester 2006

	TARGET POPULATION (n=3,400) Percentage	SAMPLE POPULATION (n=338) Percentage	DIFFERENCE Percentage Point Change
Lower Division	53%	54%	-1
Upper Division	47%	46%	+1
Total	100%	100%	

of the target population and compare that with the class standing of your sample in a table as in Figure 4.2. Note that the "difference" column shows a one percentage point difference for each, which is well within the range of consistency for even large samples and populations.

Deciding on a Method of Contact

Once the population and the sampling procedure have been determined, decide on how the respondents will be contacted. Three methods are possible: face-to-face interviews, telephone interviews, and mail/e-mail questionnaires. Each method has its own particular strengths and limitations.

Figures 4.3 and 4.4 list the advantages and disadvantages of these methods.

Informal Methods

In addition to the three formal methods, several less formal procedures for obtaining responses are also used. These include: handing out and collecting surveys at a meeting or in a class, placing the surveys at a check-in desk and asking respondents to complete the survey, or asking respondents to complete a questionnaire after they receive a service. Because you will be conducting surveys for community and government organizations, you may need to use one or a combination of these procedures to gather information.

The Internet has become another common tool for conducting surveys. Web-based surveys can be completed quickly, conveniently, and anonymously. While this method is useful if you are surveying a large group of players from different organizations, it would not be a good method for surveying a large group of stakeholders. The use of the Internet creates a sampling bias toward the members of the target population who have access to the Internet, while it ignores those who do not.

The most important advantage to these informal procedures is that they are quicker and less expensive than a ground mail, face-to-face, or telephone survey. In some cases, they have the additional advantage of being taken more seriously by the respondent because the respondents are familiar with those administering the survey and the topic may be fresher in their thinking.

However, there are serious disadvantages that depend on the type of procedure to be used.

1. If the procedure is to leave a pile of questionnaires on a table with a sign asking individuals to complete the survey, the respondents may not accurately reflect the target population. Those respondents who have lots of free time or who have the most intense (usually unfavorable) feelings about the organization are most likely to respond.

2. The response rate may be poor. The example just cited is likely to result in a low response rate unless someone administering the survey encourages or even requires people to complete the questionnaire.

3. In meeting and classroom settings, the respondents may feel coerced to answer the questionnaire and therefore may not take it very seriously or may give what they feel are the "correct" answers.

4. Never assume that it is easy to get permission to use one of these settings. You will always need to obtain the permission of the person in control of the setting (e.g., the teacher), and you may also need the approval of someone or some group higher in authority. For example, any survey conducted in the Syracuse School District must be approved by a special committee in the district.

5. Never assume that the people asked to administer the surveys will take it as seriously as you do. You need to brief them thoroughly and monitor what they do by calling immediately before they are to administer the survey. Better yet, and if possible, ask if you can administer the survey for them.

Response Rate

One of the main differences among the three methods of contact is the different **response rate** which can be obtained from each. Face-to-face contact normally yields the largest number of completed surveys, telephone contact the second largest, and mail contact the least. The usual ranges of response rates for the three types of contact are shown in Figure 4.5.

Figure 4.3: Advantages of the Three Methods of Contacting Survey Respondents

Face-to-Face	Telephone	Mail/E-mail
Chance to stimulate subject's interest	Same as face-to-face	Low cost
Supportive responses by interviewer, producing better answers	Same as face-to-face	Respondent can decide when and where to complete it
Chance to do follow-up questions, clear up ambiguous answers, answer questions in the mind of respondent	Same as face-to-face	Respondent may feel more comfortable answering personal questions in private
Responses independent of literacy or physical disabilities of respondent	Same as face-to-face	Respondent may be less threatened by mail than by direct contact

Figure 4.4: Disadvantages of the Three Methods of Contacting Survey Respondents

Face-to-Face	Telephone	Mail/E-mail
Very expensive; requires much time	Somewhat demanding of time	Respondent must take initiative to return questionaire
Dependent on skill of interviewer	Same as face-to-face	Questionnaire may be dismissed as "junk mail" unless sent first class and accompanied by personal cover letter
Respondent may be more reluctant to answer personal questions	Respondent may easily terminate survey by hanging up	Respondent may ignore some questions

Figure 4.5: Expected Ranges of Response Rates

Face-to-face	75%—90% response rate
Telephone	40%—75% response rate
Mail/E-mail	5%—50% response rate

The three methods of contact differ in other important respects besides response rate. Each of the three has particular advantages and disadvantages that you should consider in deciding which method of contact to use in your planned survey.

No matter which method of contact you use, you can do some things to increase the response rate:

- Keep the questionnaire short
- Make items easy to answer
- Use closed-choice questions
- Stimulate the interest or curiosity of the respondents
- Avoid embarrassing questions as much as possible

In any event, you must take into account an expected response rate when you decide how many members of the target population sample to contact. If you expect a 90 percent response rate, you will need to contact fewer individuals (for a given sample size) than if you expect a 10 percent response rate. The formula for estimating how many individuals to contact is to divide the desired sample size by the expected response rate, as the following formula indicates:

$$\textbf{Required contacts selected from the sampling frame} = \frac{\textbf{Desired sample size}}{\textbf{Expected response rate}}$$

For example, if you desire a sample size of 250 and you expect a response rate of 40%, the above formula (250/.40) tells you that you will need to contact 625 individuals.

Survey Ethics

In planning your survey, you need to be careful to respect the rights of the respondents. In most cases, surveys are conducted in such a way that the responses are anonymous, but in some cases, the respondents may be directly identified or the responses can be traced to them. In any case, the survey should not be done without the informed consent of the subject, the protection of the subject's right of privacy, and the protection of the confidentiality of the data. It should also not create physical, psychological, sociological, or legal risks to the respondent. Frequently, approval has to be granted by an authorized agency. For example, at many universities, an Institutional Review Board must approve all surveys that may threaten rights or collect lists. Frequently, students in high school have to receive permission by the principal to carry out any survey. Any institution that is used as a site for a survey such as a school or prison must give formal permission for the implementation of the survey. Make sure you receive approval of someone in authority before conducting the survey.

Creating the Questions

After determining the method of contacting the potential sample, your next step is to write the questions that you will use to gather your desired information. Keep the following principles in mind when creating questions:

1. Use simple and precise language with as few words as possible. This is frequently difficult to do because people attach different meaning to the same words. The KISS principle (keep it simple, stupid) is a good guide for questionnaire design.

2. Make sure the question and answer are logically consistent. For example, the following is poorly worded: *Do you live in the city or country?*

   Yes__ No__

3. Do not waste time by asking questions that respondents are unqualified to answer. Surveys are widely used to predict the outcome of elections. When correctly done, they can be good predictors. The wording in such questions is not, *Who is going to win the upcoming* election?, something that respondents might answer but which typical respondents will not be competent to judge. Instead, respondents are asked, *Whom do you support in the upcoming election?*, a response which, when asked of an appropriate sample and properly analyzed, can give a good early indicator of election results.

4. Do not ask respondents to generalize too much about their behavior, especially over time. For example, suppose you want to estimate the frequency of seat belt wearing. You might be tempted to ask a question like, *How often do you wear seat belts?*

   Always__   Sometimes__   Never__

   This asks respondents to generalize about terms that may be very inconsistently understood by different people. Another attractive but defective question would be, *How often within the last month did you wear your seat belt?*

   Survey researchers have found that individuals make very unreliable estimates when asked to generalize about their past behavior. A better way to find out about seat belt wearing, for example, is to ask the more specific question: *When you last drove your car, did you wear a seat belt?*

   Yes__   No__

   This question obtains unambiguous responses, and it asks respondents to report only their most recent behavior.

Avoid loaded or biased phrases in presenting the respondent with a question or statement. In case of controversial topics for which it is not possible to offer an objective statement, use phrasing like the following, *Some people feel..., while others feel... What is your opinion?* Choose words carefully to minimize bias.

Closed-Choice Questions

This type of question limits the kinds of answers the respondent may give, requiring a choice of one or more of the answers provided by the question.

The major advantage of closed-choice questions is that the answers given by the subjects are comparable and limited in number, making tabulating and analyzing the data much easier. In addition, this type of question requires less skill and effort on the part of the interviewer and is easier for the subject to answer. The most serious drawback is that the closed-choice question may put words in the subjects' mouths by supplying answers they may not have thought of themselves. Most subjects do not want to admit that they have not heard of an issue, and they can conceal this fact by choosing one of the answers provided.

Closed-choice questions may introduce bias, so construct them carefully. The wording and the ordering of questions and the limiting of the choice of answers can all influence the respondents' replies. As an example, consider the question: *How much do you support clean air?* _ *Slightly* _ *Moderately* _ *Strongly*

Figure 4.6: Examples of Survey Questions

There has been a great deal of concern about the rising cost of food. How do you handle the problem of rising food costs? (Check all that apply.)
    _ Purchase cheaper types of food
    _ Substitute other types of food in your daily diet
    _ Purchase large amounts of an item that is on sale
    _ Eat at restaurants less often
    _ Invite fewer people over to eat a meal at your home
    _ Don't know
    _ No answer

An example of a closed-choice scale for opinions about a proposed policy is as follows:

_ Strongly Favor   _ Favor   _ Neutral   _ Oppose   _ Strongly Oppose   _ No Answer

Still another example is this scale for obtaining information about the frequency of an activity:
    _ At least once a week
    _ Less than once a week, but at least once a month
    _ Less than once a month
    _ Never
    _ No Answer

The question introduces bias in three ways: (1) it ignores the aspect of cost or priorities such as higher taxes for clean air versus higher fuel and energy costs, (2) the choices given allow only positive responses, excluding both neutrality and opposition (closed-choice questions must allow for an equal number of responses on both sides of any issue), and (3) it does not include a choice for the failure of the respondent to answer. The options for answering must indicate all possibilities, including the respondent's failure to answer. A better question would be:

This state is presently spending $1 million per year on improving air quality. How much money do you think the government should spend?
_Much More _More _ Same _ Less _ Much Less _ No Answer

Open-ended Questions

Open-ended questions are those that allow subjects to answer the questions without restrictions imposed by the wording. Responses to open-ended questions may be extremely difficult to classify. Open-ended questions, therefore, should be used only when they are clearly appropriate. An example of an appropriate open-ended question is: "What do you think are the main causes for the rising price of food?" The most important advantage of the open-ended question is that the respondents can answer using their own reasoning and thinking patterns. In doing so, they may suggest new ideas. Another advantage is that open-ended questions do not select answers for respondents, which may be a problem with closed-choice questions. Also, this type of question can provide a chance for respondents to "warm up" at the beginning of the interview or "cool down" at the end, when respondents may be asked if there is anything else they would like to add on the topic of the survey. The major limitation to open-ended questions lies in the difficulty of making meaningful comparisons among respondents. Another problem is that interviewers require training to make sure that they conduct interviews properly. Finally, analyzing open-ended responses is more time-consuming than closed-choice responses. Whenever you decide to include open-ended questions, you must also include the specific procedures for coding the answers. Then you can make generalizations about the responses.

Estimating the Costs and Time-Table of a Survey

Surveys and interviews can be costly and time consuming. Always weigh the costs of the research with the expected benefits that the information will provide. You should never assume that time spent in doing a survey is free. Although specifying exact costs and time tables is difficult until you have had extensive experience in conducting surveys and interviews, at least be aware of immediate costs. The following should be considered:

1. *Design.* How long does the survey design take to complete? What personnel costs will be incurred?

2. *Preparation.* What costs will be required to prepare and copy the questionnaire? How long will this take?

3. *Transportation.* How much does it cost to get to respondents for face-to-face interviews, including the costs of interviewers? How long will the interviewing take?

4. *Communication.* How much does the use of the telephone or mail cost? How much time must be allocated for telephoning or receiving mail responses?

5. *Analysis.* How much time does it take to count the responses or to enter the responses in a computer and run the computer program? What costs are required for tabulating, either by hand or by computer?

6. *Report preparation.* How much time does it take and what costs are involved (e.g, typing and copying) to prepare the report?

Examining News Media Treatment of Surveys

The news media frequently report surveys relevant to public policy. When considering a published survey, keep in mind how well the news source reports on the procedures followed by the survey researchers. Some questions that should be asked of any published survey include the following:

■ For what purpose was the survey conducted and for whom was it carried out? To what specific target population are the results to be generalized?

■ What is the sample size, what is the confidence interval of the results, and how was the sample chosen?

■ What evidence is provided that the sample reflects the target population?

■ How were respondents contacted?

■ What were the key questions, and how were they worded?

■ When was the survey completed, and how long did it take for the information to be gathered?

■ What was the response rate?

Profile of a Survey Intern

Braden Lynk

Braden Lynk had no idea what he wanted to do for a career when he took PAF 101 during the first semester of his freshman year at Syracuse University. It was there that he discovered an interest in survey and data analysis, an interest that was honed in later policy studies courses. Braden took his experiences with survey research at Syracuse University into a summer internship with the polling organization Zogby International. Even though Braden was in the communications department, knowledge of surveys was crucial. He helped come up with questions for a Fourth of July poll that received a lot of media attention, with questions about the flag burning debate and other lighter questions. He also worked with opinion polling results preparing for the 2006 mid-term elections. Braden was responsible for coming up with the important results from polling in 25 'battleground states' for the elections, featuring contested Senatorial and Gubernatorial races. He then drafted the press releases for individual states. Understanding the survey process helped him explain the results accurately and in a way that the media were able to report accurately. With this internship, Braden was able to get an inside look at the workings of the increasingly important field of public opinion polling.

Chapter 5

Describing the Problem and Identifying Its Causes

"A problem well stated is a problem half solved."
— Charles F. Kettering

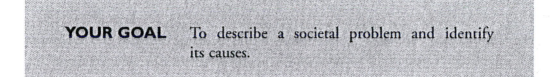

YOUR GOAL   To describe a societal problem and identify its causes.

Introduction

This chapter focuses on the analysis of a societal problem. You will be shown how to clearly describe the problem, support your assertion that the problem exists, identify the causes of the problem, and understand the existing public policies that attempt to deal with the problem. Without such analysis, you will be unable to find an effective solution to the problem.

The chapter is divided into five parts:

1.   Describing the Societal Problem

2.   Providing Evidence of the Problem

3.   Identifying Underlying Causes of the Problem

4.   Describing the Current Policy

5.   Exploring the Role of Business and Non-Profit Organizations

Part 1: Describing the Societal Problem

A good description of a societal problem contains two ingredients: (1) a clear statement of the undesirable societal condition, including the specification of its geographical setting; and (2) an indication of how the condition threatens the attainment of the six societal goals discussed in Chapter 1.

In Chapter 2 you selected a topic. You are now ready to narrow the topic into a specific societal problem. As an example of a description of a problem, consider the steps you might take in selecting an acceptable topic. You might have read or heard people talking about "crime" as a problem. This sounds like a good topic, so you begin to do some research on the topic, consulting "crime" in book and article indexes at the library.

It soon becomes clear that "crime" consists of many different societal problems. Just a few examples include international terrorism, international drug trafficking, organized crime, murder, rape, mugging, robbery, vandalism, and so-called "hate crimes" against specific groups based on their race, religion, gender, or other characteristics.

Any one of these, as well as many other specific forms of crime, is the beginning of a good description of a societal problem. Assume that you choose rape as the problem to be studied. You must also decide the setting in which to study rape. Although this is a problem in many different locations in the United States and throughout the world, you might discover that some rapes have recently been detected in your home community. Consequently, you might decide to select your local community as the geographical setting of the particular problem to be studied. The geographic setting you choose is important because this will be the setting in which you measure the problem and the level of government of your solution. Be sure to consider whether it is likely you will be able to measure the problem at this level and whether this level of government will be able to adopt a policy to reduce your societal problem.

Upon further investigation, you find that rape is a serious problem, since it not only threatens good health and personal safety, as many crimes do, but it also threatens the freedom of choice of those who are victimized.

Part 2: Providing Evidence of the Problem

Since the very existence of a problem is likely to be the source of controversy and debate, you should attempt to provide a wide range of evidence on the existence and the extent of the problem.

You can obtain several different types of evidence. Each source and type has its particular strengths and weaknesses. These are outlined below. Evidence may include combinations of the following:

1. Statistics showing change over time. If you can locate appropriate statistics, this is one of the best forms of evidence of the existence of a problem, since a societal problem is often described as something getting worse over time. However, it need not be getting worse to be a societal problem. For example, the incidence of rape may be going down in your city, but it is still considered a societal problem. One difficulty is that current statistics measuring the problem are often not available. Furthermore, some problems, such as those involving restrictions on freedom of expression, are difficult to measure with statistics. This manual requires that you choose a societal problem that can be measured quantitatively.

    A good way to present statistics is with a trend line. A trend line is a common form of graph. The trend line is derived from plotting time in years, months, or days on the x-axis (horizontal), and plotting the factor which is changing over time on the y-axis (vertical). The trend line graph shows a pattern over time for the societal problem. Figure 5.1 shows the trend from 1995 projected through 2005 on the number of deaths expected from AIDS in a hypothetical city.

    The key elements of a trend line graph are:
    a. A clear title
    b. Clear labels on both the x- and y-axis
    c. A point for each piece of data connected by a line
    d. A clear source of the information

    Be sure to include all four items in any graph you use.

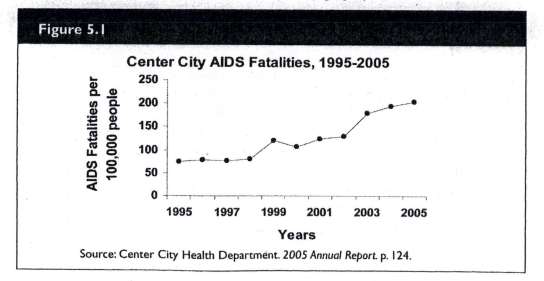

Figure 5.1

Center City AIDS Fatalities, 1995-2005

Source: Center City Health Department. *2005 Annual Report.* p. 124.

2. Statistics comparing different localities or different groups. Showing how one community, state, or nation is worse than comparable locations is also a good way to demonstrate the existence of a problem if appropriate statistics are available.

3. Views of experts. This is a useful source of evidence for many reasons. Expert interpretation of statistics is often more powerful evidence than statistics themselves. For example, while it is possible to measure air quality with great detail and sophistication, only an expert interpretation of such a measurement can be used as evidence that a problem exists. Expert judgment is also important in showing the threats to goals such as freedom of expression or freedom of choice.

4. Examples and case studies. These can be used to show detail about the nature of a problem and the effects on individuals and groups. In selecting case studies, be sure they are representative of a general situation, not unusual situations.

These four sources are generally available in books, articles, government documents, and similar publications, as described in Chapter 2. However, you may also gather information yourself.

5. You can gather information yourself through interviews (described in Chapter 3), surveys (described in Chapter 4), or observation. The advantage of doing it yourself is that the evidence can be tailored exactly to the problem and location you wish to study. The disadvantage of gathering information yourself is that it is costly and time-consuming. Even if you have the help of others, doing a good job of gathering evidence often requires careful planning, long hours of hard work, and sizable amounts of money.

Case Study

The specific societal problem we will attempt to show is that the curriculum and advising at American colleges does not adequately prepare undergraduates for a job. Evidence of the existence of the problem of the lack of job preparation by colleges can be found in several sources. The first item of evidence is a conclusion reported by Ernest L. Boyer in his book, *College: The Undergraduate Experience in America* (Boyer, 1987). Boyer's study is based on a comprehensive investigation of the conditions of undergraduate education, including extensive site visits at a sample of 29 campuses and separate surveys of faculty members, undergraduates, twelfth-grade students, parents, and academic officials (1987).

Boyer says, "...we found the baccalaureate degree sharply divided between general and specialized education. Students overwhelmingly have come to view general education as an irritating interruption—an annoying detour on their way to their degree. They all too often do not see how such requirements will help them get a job or live a life" (p. 102).

Boyer concludes that although some colleges have made concessions to the desire on the part of undergraduates for job-related courses and advice, such response has come only grudgingly and has been inadequate. Boyer summarizes the views of many faculty members when he reports that a history professor felt "deeply offended" by his college's policy of adding majors at "the whim" of local business interests (p. 106). **According to Boyer, "Many faculty members, especially those at liberal arts colleges, voiced the opinion that it is inappropriate for colleges to offer majors that are primarily 'vocational.' " Boyer quotes one science teacher who "declared that the college would be 'demeaned' if it offered programs that lead directly to a job"** (p. 108).

Boyer goes on to report that "at a small college in the Northwest, the faculty recently voted down a proposed major in computer science. 'It doesn't belong in the curriculum in the liberal arts. It's tied too closely to a job,' we were told" (p. 108).

However, colleges may need to begin offering programs that provide job training. According to a survey, the percentage of employers who say college graduates are not prepared for the workforce has increased in recent years. Figure 5.2 illustrates the results of the survey in a trend line graph.

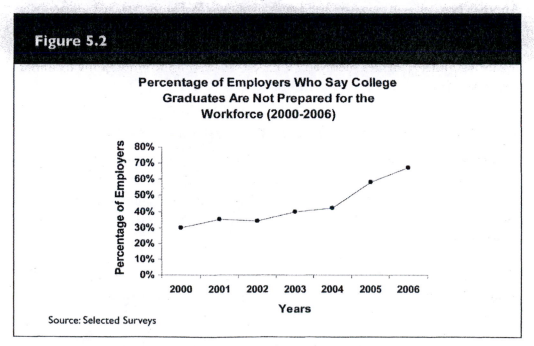

Figure 5.2

Percentage of Employers Who Say College Graduates Are Not Prepared for the Workforce (2000-2006)

Source: Selected Surveys

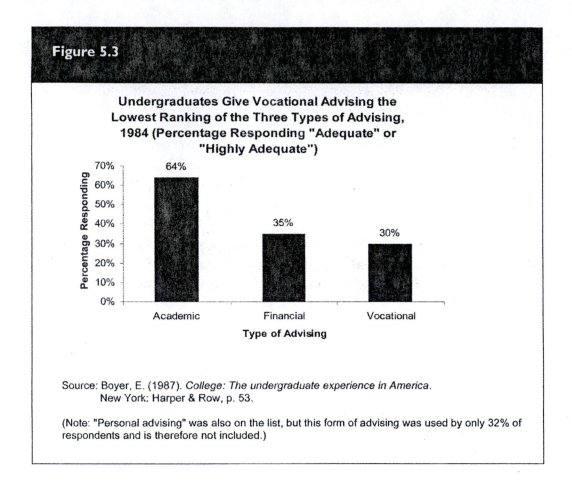

Figure 5.3

Undergraduates Give Vocational Advising the Lowest Ranking of the Three Types of Advising, 1984 (Percentage Responding "Adequate" or "Highly Adequate")

Source: Boyer, E. (1987). *College: The undergraduate experience in America.* New York: Harper & Row, p. 53.

(Note: "Personal advising" was also on the list, but this form of advising was used by only 32% of respondents and is therefore not included.)

Another item of evidence, the bar graph, is shown in Figure 5.3. It indicates that out of three major forms of advising used by students—vocational, academic, and financial—vocational has been judged the least "adequate" or least "highly adequate" by undergraduates surveyed by Ernest Boyer (p. 53) in his study of undergraduate education.

Part 3: Identifying Underlying Causes of the Problem

In this step, you will identify the reasons for the underlying factors behind the problem you have described. While the search for social, economic, and political factors can require virtually unlimited amounts of research and still may never be fully completed, you should determine those factors most clearly contributing to the problem.

To illustrate, suppose you are confronted with the problem of a growing number of burglaries in a local community. You might identify as factors contributing to the increase in the number of burglaries:

- Understaffed police force
- Increased number of wealthy households
- Inadequate security precautions
- Stricter police enforcement in neighboring communities
- Increased unemployment in the area
- Increased illicit drug usage

Developing a list of possible causes is a good way to begin thinking about possible public policies for dealing with burglaries.

Case Study

The root cause of the problem of inadequate job preparation for undergraduates is the dominant faculty culture that views with suspicion anything that smacks of too much practicality. As Boyer points out, there is much in the tradition of American and European universities that shows they have always been regarded as institutions imparting knowledge that has some practicality. Nevertheless, many faculty members ignore this aspect of the tradition and concentrate instead on the aspect of "knowledge for the sake of knowledge" with little concern for the practicality of that knowledge (Boyer, 1987, pp. 108-109).

Furthermore, faculty members apparently prefer having students who are uncertain about their career goals. Fewer than half (47 percent) of faculty reported agreement with the following statement: "In my undergraduate courses, I prefer teaching students with a clear idea of the career they will be taking (p. 107).

This unwillingness of faculty to teach material that is applied is part of a larger problem: the denigration of teaching vis a vis research. The entire process of training young graduate students to become faculty and hiring, promotion, tenure, and salary decisions are all based on this fundamental set of values. At each step along the career path, a professor's research and other activities favored by others in the professor's discipline are rewarded much more highly than activities that service the undergraduates in the professor's classes.

In his book, *Scholarship Reconsidered,* Boyer includes the results of a survey of faculty reporting that the largest change on their campuses in recent years has been the placement of a higher importance on research at the expense of teaching and service (Boyer, 1990).

In addition to attitudes of faculty and the emphasis on research rather than teaching, colleges are faced with many students who have unrealistic expectations about the kinds of jobs they may have a reasonable chance to obtain. Many want to be sports broadcasters or TV anchors or high ranking government officials when there are few openings for such positions. Most want high paying jobs and assume that they only have the options of law, medicine, or engineering. They lack the life experiences and the maturity to see the relevance of general education and skill development to their vocational pursuits. These attitudes among students are in part caused by the negative attitudes of faculty toward "practical training," but students also contribute to the problem (J. Smith, personal communication, June 13, 1992).

Part 4: Describing the Current Policy

In this step, you will learn how to describe the essential features of one of the major current policies dealing with the social problem you identified in Part 1. As described in Chapter 1, there are three elements of any public policy:

- *Legislation* to establish general guidelines
- *Executive/Administrative acts* to establish rules and to put the law into practice
- *Judicial decisions* to interpret the law in specific situations

Legislation includes both formal laws and agency regulations. For example, at the federal level, Congress establishes guidelines and approves the funding for government actions.

Administrative acts refer to all the activities that government agencies undertake to implement policies. A policy decision to increase police surveillance of roads in order to stop DWI requires many detailed decisions. These include the number of police cars, types of cars (marked or unmarked), and surveillance hours and locations. The legislation establishing the policy may require some administrative actions, but agencies almost always are allowed some freedom to make their own decisions in implementing policy.

There are three ways in which any given policy may require the outlay of funds:

- Direct cash outlays (e.g., unemployment checks)
- Purchases of goods or services (e.g., building a bridge)
- Provision of government services (e.g., police surveillance to check for DWI)

Figure 5.4: Examples of Judicial Decisions Shaping Public Policy

The Missouri Compromise, passed by Congress in 1820 to maintain an equal number of free and slave states, was declared unconstitutional in 1857 in *Dred Scott v. Sanford*.

Since the famous Supreme Court case of *Miranda v. Arizona* in 1966, police must advise a suspect of his rights at the time of arrest.

In 1974, in *U.S. v. Nixon*, the Supreme Court held that the President must obey a judge's order to provide evidence needed for a trial.

Judicial decisions take place when courts make judgments on specific cases. In some decisions, courts must interpret legislative or executive/administrative acts. Legislative and executive/administrative decisions or procedures may be declared unconstitutional if courts determine they violate the United States Constitution.

Judicial decisions can increase or decrease the force of an existing law through the strength of the penalties imposed on violators of those laws. For example, stiffer penalties for DWI, as decided by judges, are part of a policy of cracking down on drunken driving.

When examining any policy, ask the following questions to determine what elements of government actions are involved:

- What legislation underlies the policy?
- What administrative acts have been undertaken to implement the policy? What funds have been expended to implement the policy?
- Has the policy been challenged in court? What kinds of penalties have been given to violators of the law?

Information on the legislative, administrative, and judicial aspects of an existing policy can be obtained through library research and by interviewing knowledgeable people. Use the guidelines provided in Chapters 2 and 3 to obtain the information necessary to answer the questions above.

It would take years of study to acquire a comprehensive understanding of the role of public policies at the local, state, and federal levels on any significant social problem. However, public policies are always contributing factors to the existing societal problem. Even the lack of legislation for a particular problem is itself a public policy. In examining the existing policies, you are automatically looking for the causes of the problem. Usually, the policies are not the single cause or even the primary cause of a societal problem despite what some of the opponents of the policy may say. However, the policy itself needs to be considered when examining a public policy problem.

Part 5: Exploring the Role of Business and Non-Profit Organizations

While the government plays a major role in how we attempt to deal with societal conditions, other organizations are also extremely important. Two types of organizations other than the government that should be considered are businesses and non-profit organizations. Businesses influence societal conditions in both a positive and negative way. Business organizations that provide health services generally reduce poor health in our community. But, at the same time, other businesses market products such as alcohol and tobacco that threaten health.

Non-profit organizations exist to provide services either to special interest groups or to the public as a whole. The American Medical Association supports the interests of the medical profession, while the Red Cross provides services such as blood banks and disaster relief to the public at large. Non-profit organizations are incorporated just like business but the incorporation is designated as a 501(c)(3) corporation.

The solution to the complex societal conditions we all face usually requires assistance from the government (the "public sector"), business (the "private sector"), and the "non-profit" sector.

An example of the three sectors working together to address a societal problem is the movement to reduce drunk driving. Local government might step up law enforcement, bar owners might refuse to sell liquor to excessively intoxicated individuals, and Students Against Drunk Driving (SADD) might run an advertising campaign warning of the dangers of drinking and driving. When examining societal conditions, consider the role of private and non-profit organizations relative to conditions and how they would react to and be affected by public policies you would propose to address the conditions.

Profile of a Policy Analyst

Ryan Gerecht

Since this chapter is about analyzing society to identify and understand societal problems, let me introduce you to Ryan Gerecht, who graduated from Syracuse University as a Biology major in 2006 and entered Georgetown Medical School. Ryan is someone who gives back all the time. He was an EMT at the University for his entire four years and was a leader on campus. He took PAF 101 to fill one of those dreaded liberal arts core requirements at Syracuse University and chose to study the spread of HIV/AIDS in the City of Syracuse. Having a solid background in medicine gave him a start, but he soon realized that the public policy study of health issues was a lot different than medicine. He interviewed top county officials, including the County Executive, and presented a policy proposal calling for the free distribution of clean needles to drug users. The County Executive was impressed and looked into the problem because Ryan gave him hard data to show the extent and causes of the problem.

Chapter 6

Formulating a Public Policy

"You see things and say, 'Why?' But I dream things that never were, and I say, 'Why not?'"

— George Bernard Shaw

YOUR GOAL To develop public policy alternatives and provide rationale for the one you select.

Introduction

Proposing a public policy that will help to reduce the societal problem you analyzed in Chapter 5 is a difficult task. You want to propose a law or an administrative action that will work, but you also have to come up with something that key players will accept. In class, you participate in an exercise in which you negotiate with your classmates to shape the ways grades are distributed. By participating in this exercise, you will experience the process through which policy decisions are made and the tension between effectiveness and feasibility. The next section tells you how to develop three specific policy alternatives that you think will help to solve your societal problems. That is followed by a step in which you will choose one of the three alternatives. In the final step, you will examine a discussion of public policy alternatives in a newspaper article or editorial. You will be asked to determine the degree to which the writer of the article uses an approach consistent with the steps presented in this chapter.

Step 1:
Evaluating the Grading Exercise
and Increasing Learning

One type of policy by which you as a student are greatly affected is the grading policy operating in your class. How your teacher assigns grades has a significant impact on your life. The following exercise not only enables you to gain experience in the making of a policy that affects you, but it also helps you to explore the role that public and private interest goals play in shaping your behavior and the behavior of your class. The exercise gives you the opportunity to select how letter grades will be assigned to the numerical score you achieve on assignments and tests for this class. (Your teacher may choose to run this exercise as a simulation in which the results are not binding.)

In the exercise, the class will select one of three pre-determined policies aimed at dealing with a societal problem considered to be significant by the authors of this book. The problem can be described as follows: "students do not learn as much as they should from this excellent book and course." Three grading policies are considered as remedies for this problem. For the purposes of this exercise, it is assumed that all class members agree that there is a need for students to increase their level of learning in this course.

Overview

This exercise assumes that your teacher now marks according to a "Traditional System" in which letter grades are allocated in the following way:

Grade	Numerical Score
A	90–100
B	80–89
C	70–79
D	60–69
F	Below 60

After a period of class discussion, you will reach a decision as to which of the following three grading systems your class will use:

1. "Traditional System" as described above.

2. "Conservative System" in which the students who receive the top 35% of the scores receive an A; the next 15% receive a B; the next 35% receive a C; the next 10% receive a D; and the remaining 5% receive an F.

3. "Socialist System" in which the students who receive the top 10% receive an A; the next 60% receive a B; the next 15% receive a C; the next 10% receive a D; and the remaining 5% receive an F.

NOTE: If either the Conservative or Socialist System is chosen, students who would be better off with the Traditional System will receive the grade designated under the Traditional System. The Conservative and Socialist Systems are subsidies to benefit different types of students. They cannot be used to penalize students who would be better off under the Traditional System. In other words, these systems are designed to raise grades, and they will not cause anyone to receive a lower grade.

By participating in this exercise, you will learn about the way in which what is perceived to be best for the individual (increased chance of higher grades), can conflict with what is perceived as best for the class as a whole (maximum learning for everyone). This conflict between self-interest and public interest is at the heart of all policy decisions. In addition, you will gain insight into other conditions surrounding the making of public policy such as conflict between minority and majority rights, respect for others, obstacles to a responsible and representative decision, freedom of choice, and equitable rewards for talent and hard work.

Procedure

Your class will make a decision according to the following rules:

1. The final policy must be one of the Traditional, Conservative, or Socialist Systems.

2. If you fail to reach a decision by the end of the exercise, the Traditional System will stay in effect.

3. Your instructor will chair the class meeting.

4. The class can reach a decision in one of two ways:

   a. By unanimous agreement of everyone in the class selecting one of the three systems.

   OR

   b. If no unanimous agreement can be reached on one of the three systems, the class can decide on a voting procedure such as two-thirds majority, simple majority, or any other procedure. However, there must be unanimous agreement on the voting procedure.

5. Unruly behavior will result in the instructor requiring one minute of silence.

Debriefing

Once you have participated in the grading exercise, you should be able to explore the kinds of goals that motivated you, your classmates, and your instructor. Possible public interest goals include the following:

1. Promoting more learning

2. Promoting equality

3. Creating a more just system

4. Maintaining order

5. Protecting majority rights

6. Protecting minority rights

Possible private interest goals include the following:

1. Less stress

2. Less work

3. Higher grades

The kinds of goals and questions raised by the grading exercise can be found in almost every public policy issue. All public policies benefit some segments of the society and harm others, just as the Traditional System would result in lower grades for the less hardworking members of the class than would the Socialist System. The conflict between majority and minority rights developed in the exercise is similar to the conflict between the majority and minority over voting rights and equality of opportunity in the United States. To the extent that the Conservative and Socialist Systems are systems that provide subsidies to different groups, they raise questions similar to those raised about subsidies to farmers, tax credits to businesses, and tariffs on imports.

Disagreement among players in the grading exercise can also occur over means. Both sides may accept increased learning as a major goal; but those calling for a Socialist System might argue that by reducing the stress over grades, more learning would be achieved, while those calling for the Traditional System would say that competition produces more learning.

You should also recognize in your behavior and the behavior of others the relative strength of public and private interests. You may be looking for a higher grade for yourself but are putting your arguments in more public interest terms (e.g., claiming that the class would learn more). Even traditionalists, who have argued that they are only trying to preserve order, have been accused of trying to enjoy more personal satisfaction by raising the level of competition in the class.

A variety of analogies can be developed relating what happens in the grading exercise to past and current real world public policy issues. Look for the similarities and realize that policies of local, state, and federal governments will have a direct impact on goals important to you personally and to the society in which you live.

Step 2:
Developing Public Policy Alternatives

Identifying possible policies that could make a significant impact on a societal problem is a critical task. In this section, you will need to identify three alternatives. Here are some suggestions on how to develop your ideas:

1. Review existing public policies. Do any show promise but need more funding or a slightly different application? Knowledge of the success or failure of a policy may lead you to come up with a new policy.

2. Look for public policies in other cities, states, or countries that might be applied to the geographical setting of your societal problem. If you find some, consider how you would adapt them as policy alternatives for you to consider.

3. Review the factors contributing to the problem listed in Exercise 5.3. Do those factors suggest possible policies? For example, the lack of effective locks on doors is a cause of crime in dormitories. Therefore, a policy to install new locks makes a great deal of sense.

4. Ask players and experts what they think would be effective policies.

5. Study proposals made in legislatures, government reports, and academic studies.

In selecting the three alternatives, consider two criteria:

Effectiveness: Select the policies most likely to have a major impact on reducing the societal problem.

Political Feasibility: Select the policies most likely to be accepted by key players.

Unfortunately, policies that are high on one are often low on the other. For example, capital punishment for drug traffickers in the United States would probably be effective in reducing the use of illegal drugs; however, it would not be feasible because political opposition to such a law would be so great. Your three alternatives should be reasonable on both criteria. In general, feasibility is the more important criterion. It is usually easy to think of many extreme policies that would be effective, but they are useless because they are not feasible. Policies that have a reasonable chance of being accepted (even if they are only partially effective) are generally the preferred alternatives.

WARNING ABOUT COMING UP WITH THE RIGHT AGENCY FOR YOUR PROPOSAL: Because we live in a federal system, the agency that will implement your public policy is not always easy to figure out. It could operate at the local, state, or federal level, but the big problem is that each level may actually have a hand in it. For example, if you wanted to improve readings levels in elementary schools by implementing a new reading program, it would probably be a school district policy for a given area like a city. However, the state and federal government may play a role by providing funds or requiring certain testing to improve reading. Be sure to research carefully the level of government and government agency that has the authority to implement your policy proposal. If you want to propose a free after-school tutoring program, you may want to propose a federal policy or state policy.

Step 3:
Choosing the Preferred Alternative

Once you have identified three alternatives, you will need to explain which of the three you prefer. Your choice must weigh the two criteria mentioned above—effectiveness and political feasibility. The example below may be helpful:

Figure 6.1: Example of How to Weigh Feasibility and Effectiveness

Alternate Policies for Reducing DWI:

1. Establish a federal minimum drinking age of 21 years. (AGE)

2. Make all new cars sold have a feature where the driver must pass a breathalizer test in order to start the car. (TEST)

3. Make the consumption of alcohol illegal. (CONS)

		Feasibility		
		High	Medium	Low
Effectiveness	High		AGE	CONS
	Medium		TEST	
	Low			

The 21-year-old drinking limit (AGE) is the preferred choice, because it is more feasible than the other two and is at least as effective as the other two. It has medium feasibility, because many states dislike federal intrusion in this area. It is highly effective because it reduces the number of DWI arrests where it is the law. Testing (TEST) has a medium level of effectiveness, because it would slightly reduce the number of drunken drivers. Because of its extremely high cost, it is low on feasibility. Making consumption illegal (CONS) is high on effectiveness, because it would reduce the number of drunk drivers. However, it is low on feasibility; prohibition was already tried in this country and proved to be very unpopular.

Although you do not have to present the diagram in completing Step 3, you should use it to assess the three alternatives you consider. You will find it useful to draw it and place the three alternatives in the appropriate cells to help you develop your reasoning for selecting the preferred alternative.

Step 4:
Examining the News Media's Treatment
of Policy Proposals

The news media allows players and their audiences to express their views on preferred public policies. It may broadcast or report a policy proposal by a major player, such as the President or a member of Congress. The most elaborate presentations are usually found in the editorial pages of newspapers where space is provided for advocates.

A review of the editorial pages of newspapers will reveal that policies are not usually presented in the systematic manner suggested by Steps 2 and 3. Rarely does a writer list three possible policy alternatives and argue in a balanced way why the preferred alternative is better on the basis of effectiveness and feasibility. More often, writers will provide only a simple proposal and provide one-sided support for it.

Profile of Policy-Maker

John Mandyck

John Mandyck graduated from Syracuse University in 1989 as a Policy Studies major after a remarkable career as a student leader. John always had it together, even as a high school senior when he visited the SU campus, not to check out the dorms, but to interview the author of this manual, Bill Coplin, as the director of the Policy Studies program. John was elected President of the Student Government as a sophomore and ran a very successful administration. His most remarkable achievement was to get the Chancellor to meet with the Syracuse City Mayor to work a deal in which a road on the main campus was shut down to outside traffic. People were getting hit by cars on a regular basis, and John came up with a policy to reduce traffic. John went on to a remarkable business career and is now Vice President for Government Relations with the Carrier Corporation.

Chapter 7

Examining the Benefits and Costs of a Policy

"Laws are written for the lofty aim of the 'common good' and then acted out in life on the basis of common greed." —— Saul Alinsky

YOUR GOAL   To identify and rate the benefits and costs of a policy.

Introduction

This chapter introduces you to the task of estimating, measuring, and rating the expected benefits and costs of a policy if it is implemented. The previous chapter discussed formulating public policy. In that chapter, you considered alternative policies to deal with a societal problem and selected one of those alternatives. As that chapter indicated, a reasoned choice is based on your expectation of which of the alternatives will be most politically feasible and most effective. In this chapter, you will make more careful estimates of the expected future effectiveness of your policy. The next chapter will show you how to make a more systematic forecast of one of the benefits. Later chapters will deal with feasibility.

A careful consideration of a policy's effectiveness means making estimates of both the future desirable consequences of a policy, called "benefits," and the future undesirable consequences of a policy, called "costs." An effective policy is one which produces benefits that clearly outweigh its costs.

Examining a policy's benefits and costs should be done when formulating a policy. Weighing the benefits and costs of different policy alternatives helps you to decide which alternative is best from the standpoint of effectiveness. Once you have chosen a policy alternative, you can use its benefits and costs to convince others to support your policy.

In policy-making situations, policies that have been implemented in past years are studied to identify what benefits and costs they have actually produced. This process of studying the desirable and undesirable effects of a previously implemented policy is called "evaluation."

Evaluation is an essential task of public policy analysis because it measures the effectiveness of the policy selected. Unfortunately, it is a task not frequently carried out in a systematic way. Usually, policy-makers are so consumed in debating which policies to follow and how to implement them that they lack the time or energy to assess the impact of the policy itself. It is important that public policy analysts develop skills in evaluating policies.

Failure to evaluate policies hurts policy-making in several ways:

- Policies that do not work may be continued

- Policies that do work may be abandoned

- Potential lessons from our mistakes are lost

- Policy-makers are not held accountable for what they do

The skills you acquire in this chapter prepare you for beginning a policy evaluation study.

Identifying Benefits

Benefits are consequences of a policy that you consider to be good for the society or some segment of it. For example, the primary benefits of mandatory seat belt laws are fewer fatalities and injuries to those involved in automobile accidents.

Benefits can be tangible, usually expressed in the form of dollars or other numbers. For example, seat belt laws might eventually reduce car insurance by an average of $30 to $50 per year and decrease fatalities by about 10 percent. Benefits can also be intangible and hard to measure concretely. For example, drivers and passengers may feel more secure wearing seat belts. Both tangible and intangible benefits are important to consider in evaluating an existing or proposed public policy.

The city government decides to take action against increased vandalism by youths. It implements a policy of hiring 100 youths to patrol the city parks. The benefits include:

- The action itself: the 100 jobs.

- An intended consequence of the policy: reduction of vandalism.

- An unintended consequence of the policy: increased enjoyment of the park by more people as the park's appearance is improved by the reduced vandalism.

The best way to assess the benefits of a policy is to use the six goals listed in Figure 1.1 which are derived from the phrase "life, liberty, and the pursuit of happiness." Each of these goals may give you an idea of what benefits might occur for society as a result of this policy.

Three sources of benefits are:

- The action itself
- The intended consequences of the policy
- The unintended consequences of the policy

The first category applies only when the policy itself represents a benefit. Intended and unintended consequences are less easy to identify. Intended consequences are, in effect, the goals of the policy. Unintended consequences are indirect results of the policy, changes produced that are not the goals of the policy but are produced by the policy nevertheless.

Identifying Costs

Costs are consequences of a policy that are undesirable for either the society as a whole or some segment of it. For example, the primary costs of the mandatory seat belt laws are a loss of freedom of choice for drivers and passengers and more law enforcement expenditures.

Costs, like benefits, can be tangible, usually expressed in the form of dollars or other quantities. For example, a community's budget for additional law enforcement may increase by $10,000, a 2 percent increase. They can also be intangible and hard to measure concretely. For example, more hostile attitudes toward government may result from the seat belt requirement. Both tangible and intangible costs are important to consider.

Costs have the same three sources as benefits:

- The action itself
- The intended consequences of the policy
- The unintended consequences of the policy

In taking the action of employing 100 youths to patrol the city parks, the city government will incur costs, in addition to the benefits cited in the section, "Identifying Benefits." The costs include:

■ The action itself: the salary of the youths.

■ An intended consequence: salary of additional staff to supervise the 100 new employees.

■ An unintended consequence: more litter and increased wear and tear on the park from increased usage.

In some cases, costs can be the opposite of originally forecast benefits. For example, because people are wearing seat belts, they may feel overly secure and drive more recklessly. A resulting cost may be increased traffic deaths instead of the expected reduction in traffic deaths.

Costs should be examined relative to the six goals inherent in Jefferson's phrase "life, liberty, and the pursuit of happiness." In general, the costs of some policies are often related to the loss of freedom of choice due to the required new behavior. Sometimes a loss of economic opportunity may be involved if the policy requires paying higher taxes or having additional costs of doing business.

Comparing Benefits and Costs

Not all benefits and costs are equally important in choosing a preferred policy alternative. You must first decide which benefits and costs are more important than others before you can select one policy alternative over another. The only reasonable policy alternatives are those that have a good chance of resulting in more benefits than costs.

The following procedure is a simple method for calculating a benefit-cost ratio. Using it will help you choose among a set of alternatives. The first step is to assign a weight to each cost and benefit based on its importance. Decide if you feel that the importance of each expected effect is "high," "medium," or "low." This judgment will not necessarily be accepted by others, because these are estimates about an uncertain future. Furthermore, people often differ strongly about the importance of different consequences. But if you are clear about your rating, at least this will help you in your own analysis. Your rating may also help you communicate clearly with others.

In the policy of hiring 100 youths to patrol the city parks, a planned benefit was reduction of vandalism in the parks. However, vandalism could increase because some of the hired youths could take advantage of their access to the park and increase the vandalism.

Assign a "high" rate to those benefits or costs that you believe will seriously affect several of the six goals. Assign a "moderate" rate to those benefits or costs that you estimate will have a slight effect on several of the six goals or a moderate effect on one goal. Assign a "low" rate to those benefits or costs that have just a slight effect on one or two of the goals. To help clarify the rating and to help reach a conclusion about the relative benefits and costs, translate the rates into numbers as follows:

Rating of Benefit or Cost	Numerical Score
High	3
Medium	2
Low	1

This helps show not only how each benefit or cost rates, but it also shows how to calculate the ratio of benefits to costs as you have estimated them. The procedure is as follows: add the totals of all benefits. Then add the totals of all costs. Divide the benefit total by the cost total to obtain a benefit-cost ratio. If this ratio is greater than 1.0, the benefits outweigh the costs, and the policy is worth pursuing. If the ratio is exactly 1.0 (the benefits exactly equal costs) or less than 1.0 (the costs outweigh the benefits), the policy is not worth pursuing.

Case Study

Consider a proposed policy of providing educational programs on crime prevention to members of residence halls in order to reduce larcenies. This policy has several benefits and costs, each listed below with the rankings assigned to each depending on our assessment of whether their level of importance is "high," "medium," or "low."

Benefits	Score	Costs	Score
Reduction in larcenies	3	Staff costs	2
Increased personal safety	2	Printing	1
More work for staff	1	Loss of freedom	1

Of the three benefits, the most important is reduction in larcenies (ranked 3). The increased personal safety (ranked 2), while somewhat important, is ranked only moderate, because larcenies represent only a slight threat to personal safety. The benefit of increased work for staff (ranked 1) is only minor, since other important work could be found for the staff if they were not engaged in the educational program.

Payment for staff (ranked 2) is the most important cost, but it is only moderately important, since most of the staff would be paid to do other things if not conducting the programs. The printing costs (ranked 1) are very low, less than $200. The loss of freedom (ranked 1) is also of only low importance because, although loss of freedom is very important, being required to sit through a crime-prevention session is a very minor restriction on freedom.

To estimate the benefit-cost ratio of this proposed policy, first add the scores of all the benefits (3+2+1=6), then add the scores of all the costs (2+1+1=4). Next divide the sum of the benefits by the sum of the costs (6/4=1.5). The resulting number (1.5 in this case) is the "benefit-cost ratio." When this ratio is greater than 1.0 (as it is in this case), this means that the estimated future benefits outweigh the estimated future costs of the proposed policy, and the policy is therefore worth pursuing. If this ratio is exactly 1.0, it indicates that the benefits and costs are exactly equal. If the ratio is less than 1.0, it indicates that the costs outweigh the benefits. In these latter two cases, the policy would not be worth pursuing.

Analyzing Benefit-Cost Discussion in the News Media

The criticism presented on the one-sidedness of policy presentations also applies to the benefits and costs of a policy. Editorials and supporters of specific policies rarely look at both the costs and the benefits and discuss ways of systematically measuring each. They neither prioritize among the benefits and costs nor seek to come up with a benefit-cost ratio. However, good journalists—more often in the print media, though sometimes in the electronic media—will attempt to present a view of both sides of an issue. It is useful to compare the positions of various commentators on a given policy in terms of the benefits and costs they identify and the weights they assign to them. A careful study of these views would lead to conclusions about the entire range of benefits and costs related to a specific policy proposal.

Profile of a Benefit-Cost Queen

Renee Captor

Renee Captor was a student of mine in the late 1970s who became a successful defense lawyer in the City of Syracuse. In 2002, she took over a county job of running an agency that placed assigned counselors with people who could not afford a lawyer. She now manages a multi-million dollar budget to support lawyers she hires on a fee basis to help poor people. She uses her skills as a policy analyst, including spreadsheet analysis, to make decisions about which lawyers to hire and assign. She is careful to balance the benefit of helping the poor with the cost to taxpayers.

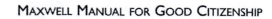

Chapter 8

Benchmarking Public Policy

"Everyone is entitled to his own opinion, but not his own facts."
— Daniel Patrick Moynihan

YOUR GOAL Use benchmarks to develop a plan to help determine the success of your policy.

Introduction

Benchmarking is like using a thermometer when you think you have a fever. Your temperature tells you where you are so you can compare that measurement with where you want to be. If you are not meeting your goal (normal body temperature or 98.6° F), you take remedial action, or in this case, two aspirin.

When it comes to public policy, benchmarking is a way to assess the effectiveness of your policy. In Chapter 6, you chose a policy that was both effective and feasible. We will talk about feasibility in the next chapter. Benchmarking is a way to tell if your policy is at least somewhat effective. If, after your policy is implemented, societal conditions improve to a certain point (the benchmark), your policy is effective.

Benchmarks consist of two parts: (1) indicators that measure some condition, and (2) a goal for that condition. Benchmarks are best thought of as measurable objectives. To adapt what David Osborne and Ted Gaebler said in *Reinventing Government*, when they described some benefits of evaluation (1993, pp. 146-155):

■ What gets benchmarked gets done.

- If you do not benchmark results, you cannot tell success from failure.

- If you cannot recognize failure to reach benchmarks, you cannot improve performance.

- If you cannot see success, you cannot learn from it.

- If you can demonstrate results, you can win public support.

The last benefit must be emphasized at the outset. Getting a clear fix on the current situation and future goal in measurable terms can serve to rally your troops and create a target about which all can agree. Building widespread support for benchmarks is necessary for creating effective public policies. It has worked wonders in business and is starting to do the same in government and the nonprofit world.

Benchmarks are basically goals that can be clearly measured. They usually consist of an indicator of the way things are and a hoped-for indicator of where we want them to be. For example, the crime rate for a city is 10 reported crimes per 1,000 of population for 1999; you might set as a benchmark that it be reduced to eight reported crimes per 1,000. You must measure the condition and then decide what level would be considered acceptable.

Sometimes the measurement need not be quantitative; it could also be qualitative. A benchmark for a police department in New York State could be that it is certified by the State of New York. Believe it or not, many police departments in New York State are not certified. This chapter will describe only quantitative benchmarks. For a full discussion of both quantitative and qualitative benchmarks, see *Does Your Government Measure Up?: Basic Tools for Local Officials and Citizens* by William D. Coplin and Carol Dwyer (2000).

8.1: Identifying Quantitative Data to Use Your Benchmark

The first and key step for using benchmarks is to measure through quantitative data the societal conditions that you believe will be improved in your proposed policy. This can be either a desirable societal condition that will be increased by your proposed policy (percent graduating high school) or an undesirable societal condition that will be decreased by your policy (dropout rate).

After deciding what key societal condition you want to benchmark, obtain a quantitative indicator, or variable, that measures the condition for the last four consecutive calendar years. For example, the benefit of a law requiring that air bags be placed in all cars might be measured by the variable of "traffic deaths per

100 million miles driven" for each of the four years prior to the implementation of the law. The expectation is that this variable would show a decline after the law is implemented.

In looking at historical trends, the general rule is the longer the time period examined the better. Professional policy analysts would typically look at a period of ten years. A minimum of four years is sufficient at this stage in your development as a policy analyst.

Choose a variable for which you can obtain enough data for four recent time periods ending in the last full calendar year (e.g., if it is September 2007, your last year should be 2006). Make sure that the variable is a reasonable measure of the societal condition your policy seeks to improve. The time interval that is usually used is a year, but if you are doing academic programs, you may want to use the academic year (e.g., 2001-2002). If you are looking at something like the environment or health conditions, you may want to use five or ten year intervals. Regardless of what time interval you choose, be sure the length of each interval is consistent.

The variable you select should be scaled in some way. This means that instead of saying there were 25 murders in the City of Syracuse last year, you would say there were 3 murders per 100,000 people. Or instead of saying that 200 students dropped out of school, you would say the dropout rate is 10 percent. Avoid using absolute numbers. For more information about scaling numbers, see Chapter 16. In many cases, you will be unable to obtain data for the most recent year(s). If this occurs, provide an estimate and give a rationale for that estimate. Indicate that the number is an estimate by placing an "e" next to the year. In some cases, you will be able to find data for part of a year as the basis for an estimate. In other cases, the estimate will be based on your best judgment, including estimates by knowledgeable people and the pattern over the years for which you have real data.

Case Study

Consider a proposed policy to educate college dormitory residents about proper security measures in order to alleviate the societal problem of the number of larcenies in college dormitories.

The information provided below is based partially on information about a real university, which we call Citrus University. This university has 10,000 students. There were 1,230 larcenies in 2004, but we are scaling it to be per 1,000 students to make the math easier. Therefore, there were 123 larcenies per 1,000 students in 2004, which is shown on Figure 8.1. This data was collected in 2007, but we lacked the real data for 2007, so we estimated the statistics for that year.

Figure 8.1: Data on the Number of Larcenies in Residence Halls at Citrus University per 1,000: 2004-2007

Time Period	Number of Larcenies	Source or Rationale
2004	136	Citrus Univ. Security Dept. Annual Report, 2004
2005	123	Citrus Univ. Security Dept. Annual Report, 2005
2006	142	Citrus Univ. Security Dept. Annual Report, 2006
2007e	126	Between January and June 2007, 63 larcenies were reported. The estimate was made for all of 2007 by doubling that number because about the same number of larcenies occur in each six month period.

8.2: Calculating Percent Change Using Excel*

*Note: These instructions apply specifically to Microsoft Excel XP, but any spreadsheet program has similar features. Look for the key terms like "Format cells" or "Wrap text."

In order to see if a pattern exists in your data, you need to determine the "percent change" between years. The past pattern will help you understand how much change you can expect from your policy. Percent change gives you a precise indicator of the amount of change from one year to the next. Using the data listed in Figure 8.1, you will need to calculate four percent changes:

1. Between the 1st and 2nd year

2. Between the 2nd and 3rd year

3. Between the 3rd and 4th year

4. Between the 1st and 4th year

The last percent change will help you get a bigger picture of the pattern.

Percent change is very useful for many things, not just public policy. You can use it to determine what percent raise you get between this year and the previous year. You can compare two different things, like the percent difference between two prices for a car or a loan. For public policy, it is essential because changes in societal conditions are frequently small, and looking at how big a change there is percent wise is instructive on whether or not your policy is having an impact.

This step tells you how to calculate a percent change with a calculator (or by hand if you are good at mental arithmetic) and also by using Microsoft Excel.

Calculating Percent Change

To have a clear understanding of what percent change means, you should practice the hand calculations a few times. Moreover, you may not always have an Excel program available to you when you want to make the calculation.
Use the following formula:

Percent change = [(New figure - Old figure) / Old figure] x 100

The percent change calculations for larcenies at Citrus University from 2004 to 2005 are:

-9.56% = ((123-136)/136)x100.

The formula compares the old figure by subtracting from the new figure. By dividing the remainder by the old figure, you can determine how much or by what percent the new figure changed. See Figure 8.3 for our Citrus University case study example.

Using Excel

Fortunately, you can use Microsoft Excel to do your calculations for you. Excel is used in business, government, and the nonprofit sector. No one should leave college without learning Excel. This section is written for a person who has no familiarity with Excel.

Here are the steps you must follow:

- You need to find a computer that has Excel. Some Mac computers have Excel if Microsoft Office is installed on the computer. Once the computer is booted up and the desktop comes up, click on the Excel Program. It is part of Microsoft Office.

- The document you are working on is called a workbook. The workbook is comprised of one or more worksheets within the document. In a workbook, one worksheet could be a table, the next a chart, and the next a graph; but they would all be based on the same data.

- Each **column** is represented by a letter.

- Each **row** is represented by a number.

- Each **cell** is represented by a letter and a number combination (A4).

- Each **field** is represented by the cell names separated by a colon (A4:A10).

- You can select a cell to enter data into by clicking on it.

- To format cells, you can go to **Format** on the toolbar and click **Format cells**.

- When you are done typing the data in, you can press **Enter** or any of the **arrow keys** on the keyboard to move to another cell.

- When you put the mouse cursor (the arrow) over any of the buttons at the top of the screen, words will appear underneath to tell you what the button is for. These buttons are "shortcuts" to help you perform many of the common functions used in Excel.

- When you want to use one of the button functions, you select the appropriate cell or highlight the cells and then click on the button.

- If you enter numbers, they will automatically right justify. If you enter text, it will automatically left justify. If you enter any combination of numbers and letters, it will left justify. This can easily be changed by highlighting the data and selecting the appropriate justify button.

1. Enter the title of the table in cell A1. To fit more text in a cell, you can make its height greater while not making it wider. To do this: **highlight** the cell itself (not the information in the cell), right click on your mouse, click on **Format Cells**, go to the **Alignment** tab, and check off **Wrap Text**. Otherwise, your title will extend into more than one cell.

2. In order to allow your title cell to run into more than one column in width (i.e., A1, B1, C1), **highlight** the cells you wish to extend over, **right click** your mouse, click on **Format Cells**, go to the **Alignment** tab, and click on **merge cells**.

3. Now, enter your column headings in row 4 in each consecutive cell. Adjust the column width to make the headings fit.

   a. To automatically adjust the column width, move the arrow between the gray letter headings until it changes shape to a vertical bar with two arrows pointing either way horizontally. Then, double click your mouse and it will become as wide as the longest text written in the column.

b. To manually adjust the column width, press the mouse button down when the cursor changes shape and drag the mouse either way while keeping the button pressed. Let go when it's the size you want.

c. The same applies for adjusting the **row height**.

4. **Center** the year and number columns headings. To do this: **highlight** the area that you want to center and then **click** on the toolbar shortcut button with the lines that look centered. This button is in between the buttons to left and right justify. To alter the vertical position of data, **right click** on the cell, click **Format Cells**, go to the **Alignment** tab, and change vertical setting to **Center**.

5. **Bold face** the title and the column headings. Highlight the cells you want boldfaced. Then, click on the toolbar shortcut button with the large **B**. Your goal is to create a table that is similar to the example with your data.

6. To prepare your table so it has specific gridlines, you have to highlight the table in separate sections. You want the gridlines to distinguish the columns, but not the rows (with the exception of the column headings). Highlight those cells you want to affect. Right click and choose **Format Cells**. Click the **Border** tab and select from the menu the sides of the highlighted cells you would like to show gridlines (i.e., outline, inside, left, right, bottom, etc.). Remember that you may have to highlight different fields and perform this action multiple times to achieve the same gridlines as in the example.

7. In the "Percent Change" column, you are using formulas to get the correct percent. The program does the math for you. Again, make sure you follow the exact format and put the appropriate values in. If you have spaced everything like the example, you should be entering the exact formula.

8. Once you have entered the formulas and pressed Enter, you should see the number that is a result of the formula. You may need to reduce the number of decimal places you see. To do this: **highlight** the column of percents and then press one of the two shortcut buttons (or go to **Format** on the toolbar menu, **format cells**, **number** tab) in the toolbar with .00 and an arrow going either way on them.

These will increase or decrease the amount of decimal places shown. Press the shortcut button that will decrease your number to one decimal place. If these buttons do not appear in your toolbar, press the small button on the far right that has two arrows and a down arrow. You can choose to add these two shortcuts to your toolbar for convenience.

9. Now you need to change your numbers to percents. To do this: **highlight** the cells that have decimals in them to be converted to percents. **Right click** on your mouse and select **Format Cells** and click on the **Number** tab if it does not automatically go to it. Click on **Percentage** and type **"1"** into the box that says "Decimal Places." Then click **OK** and when you get back to your spreadsheet, you should see your decimals displayed as percentages.

The comparison between the first and last year should be in the last row and also uses a formula. Type the formula into the cell using the appropriate values.

These are the formulas you should enter in your table exercise:

Figure 8.2

	A	B	C
1	Percent Change for Larceny at Citrus University By Excel		
2			
3	Time Period	Number of Larcenies Per 1,000 Students	Percent Change
4	2004	136	
5	2005	123	=((B5-B4)/B4)x100
6	2006	142	=((B6-B5)/B5)x100
7	2007e	126	=((B7-B6)/B6)x100
8			
9	Compare 2004 to 2007e		=((B7-B4)/B4)x100

Figure 8.3 shows what the print out will look like if you do it correctly.

By calculating the percent change, you will be able to see better the pattern in the societal condition you hope your policy will improve. Basically, you will find one of three patterns (if there is a pattern):

1. A steady increase

2. A steady decrease

Figure 8.3

Percent Change for Larceny at Citrus University		
Time Period	**Number of Larcenies per 1,000 Students**	**Percent Change**
2004	136	
2005	123	-9.6%
2006	142	15.4%
2007e	126	-11.3%
Compare 2004 to 2007e		-7.4%

Source: Citrus Univ. Security Dept. Annual Report, 2004-2006.

3. Up and down

Or there may be no clear pattern. Looking at the percent change from year to year will help you determine the pattern. Examining the percent change between the first and fourth year will tell you if there is any longer-term change. If it is close to zero, there is no long-term change for the four-year period, even if there is from year to year.

Case Study

Figure 8.3 above records the percent change for larcenies in Citrus University residence halls. It shows wide swings in the larceny levels, meaning that the levels are up and down. This is usually called a cyclical pattern. The table shows that the percent change between the first and fourth year, in addition to the changes each year, is –7.4 percent. In this case, the percent change is misleading because there is no trend.

8.3: Deciding on the Years to Use for Your Benchmark

Now that you have your data for the recent past and you have an understanding of the pattern (if any) between the years, your next step is to choose the date when you would expect your benchmark to be reached. How many years will the policy have to be in effect before your policy can reach its benchmark? Some policies have an immediate effect but lose their impact over time. Some policies take time to go into effect. You will need to look at the pattern you discovered in 8.2, as well as your entire analysis in Chapters 5 and 6, to figure this out.

Come up with a benchmark for at least three different time periods using the same time intervals as you used in 8.2. This will help you decide whether or not your policy has a lasting effect. You can start in the next calendar year or wait as long as five years into the future to start. No matter how long you wait, the three years chosen should be in the same time intervals as your historical data. Usually, you should choose the next three calendar years so the results can be measured immediately.

You must also check your benchmark each year for at least a three-year period. This will help reduce the chance of reaching a conclusion based on a "fluke" year. You may want to have different benchmark numbers for each year showing progressive improvement, or you can set one benchmark that you hope will be reached each of the three years.

Once you have decided on the three different years your benchmark should be reached, you are ready to choose a level.

8.4: Making a Baseline Forecast

To help you choose a benchmark and demonstrate the impact of your policy, you will need to estimate what the levels of your variable will be for the three years you have decided to benchmark **if there were no policy change**. We call this the **"baseline forecast."**

Developing Your Baseline Forecast

To come up with a baseline forecast of what the trend would be if the policy were not implemented for each of the three years you chose in 8.3, you need to consider several things. An examination of the past trend through visual inspection, as well as the percent change calculated in 8.2, will help you make your baseline forecast.

Unfortunately, there is no magic formula for making a forecast of this kind. The best you can do is to think hard and examine all the information you can to come up with a forecast. Begin by asking if there is a consistent pattern in the historical data, and decide whether what has happened in the past will continue into the future. The pattern can be increasing, decreasing, or staying the same. Depending on the answer, you can use the following rules to make your forecast.

If you decide that the pattern is consistent, then:

1. Assume that the pattern will be similar for the years you are forecasting.

2. If the increase or decrease has been steady and uniform, you can continue the exact percent change. For example, if the increase in reading scores is 3 or 4 percent downward during the four years in your historical data, use 3 or 4 percent to make your forecast.

3. More likely, though, the increase or decrease will not be uniform, and you will have to use either the average or median percent change, whichever makes more sense for your data set. You can obtain the average percent change by finding the sum of the percent change for each year, then dividing by the number of years. You can obtain the median percent change by finding the percent change that is the middle number, or the average of the two middle numbers, in your sequence of numbers for percent change.

4. If you do decide to use this reasoning, you are obliged to explain why you expect the same percent change to continue.

If the pattern is inconsistent, then:

1. Follow the ups and downs in the previous four years.

2. The average changes for your three years should be close to the average of changes for your three predicted years.

There are also conditions where it is incorrect to assume that what has happened in the past will continue in the future in a baseline forecast. Therefore, consider the following factors:

1. Special events or conditions. A major outside event or related societal condition such as a rise in prices or shift in the economic growth may produce a different forecast.

2. The trend may be approaching an outer limit. For example, the literacy rate in a country may grow 3 percent a year if it is below 50 percent, but if literacy is approaching the 80 percent level, the annual change would probably slow down because the last group of individuals who are illiterate would be the most difficult to make literate.

3. Demographic factors—size and age of population may affect societal conditions. For instance, an older population could lead to lower crime rates and birth rates.

4. Many societal conditions tend to be cyclical or self-correcting, so a period of major increase may be followed by a period of stabilization or decline. Slower economic growth in two or three years tends to be followed by somewhat faster economic growth the following years because people will eventually buy the products they wanted but did not buy in the earlier period. If the cyclical pattern is year by year as discussed above, use the same pattern, but sometimes the cycle is much longer.

Make your forecast using the guidelines above. When you justify your forecast, clearly list each of the factors you think may lead to an increase or decrease of the variable in the future. The forecast you present will be, in fact, your judgments concerning the net results of all these factors. Also indicate in your justification how your baseline forecast is similar to, or differs from, the historical trend.

Using a Trend Line Graph

Displaying your baseline forecast through a trend line graph is a good way to present ideas about the future. Using the forecasts generated by the analysis described above, create a trend line graph similar to the one in Figure 8.4 created for the case study of Citrus University. This section presents the graph and a justification for the forecast. It is followed by detailed directions on how to insert a trend line graph into a paper. For more information on trend line graphs, see Chapter 16.

Case Study

The baseline forecast presented in Figure 8.4 is based on the historical trend between 2004 and 2007. That trend shows a cyclical pattern with no major increase or decrease over four years.

There are a few factors that cause the cyclical pattern in larcenies. The main factor leading to a decrease in the number of larcenies is student concern resulting from the history of high levels of larcenies in dormitories. The strength of this factor will vary from year to year. It is highest when the level of larcenies has peaked and lowest when the level has dropped. The main factor preventing the larcenies from dropping substantially is the continuation of poor economic conditions of the residents who live near the campus. Another factor keeping the number of larcenies high is the use of alcohol and other drugs by both students and neighboring residents.

In 2008, the larceny rate should increase to 136 larcenies. Because of the low level of larcenies the year before (126), complacency on the part of both students and security officials will produce a high larceny level. Additionally, drug and alcohol use by students and neighboring residents will contribute to an increase in larcenies throughout the entire three-year period because there is currently no effective policy to deal with drugs and alcohol.

In 2009, the larceny rate will decrease to 122 larcenies because of the residents' concerns from previous high larceny levels. In addition, the poor economic conditions surrounding the campus, one of the main reasons for the larcenies, will ease somewhat as the city government is introducing an economic development project in the area. However, since this project is just starting, a large number of resi-

Figure 8.4

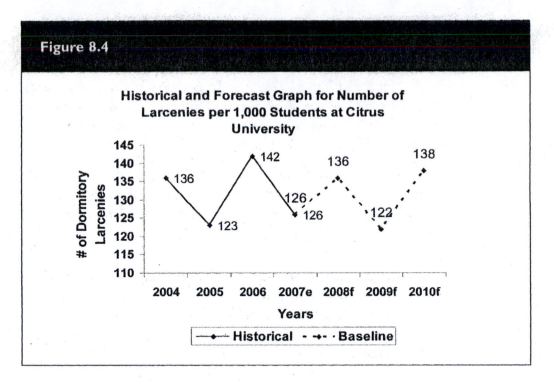

Historical and Forecast Graph for Number of Larcenies per 1,000 Students at Citrus University

dents will remain unemployed in 2009 and 2010, and the effect of the project on the number of larcenies will be modest.

In 2010, the number of larcenies will increase to 138. Again, complacency on the part of students and security officials will play a major role in this increase. The frustration of neighboring residents will increase because they will not see the immediate effect of the economic development project that they had hoped for. This will also lead to an increased level of larcenies.

Note that the percent change from the historical data was not used to make the baseline forecast because no consistent pattern was evident. The historical data showed a cyclical pattern, so that method of reasoning was used to make predictions along with special circumstances that did not exist in the past, such as the implementation of a new economic development project.

Inserting a Trend Line Graph

You will need to insert a trend line graph for your own historical data and baseline forecast. Follow these steps to insert a graph into your Microsoft Word document. Directions for trend graph (Using Word 2003, other versions might vary slightly):

1. Under "Insert" on the main toolbar, select "picture" and then "chart." A bar graph will appear with default values and formatting. A table will also

open. This table is the data source. The default usually has four columns (labeled 1st Qtr, 2nd Qtr, etc.) and three rows (East, West, North). Change the columns to be your time periods (typically years) and the rows to be "Historical" and "Baseline." To get the last row to disappear, put your cursor next to the "3," which is in the gray box to the left of the cell labeled "North." A white cross should appear, and then double-click. The entire row should turn light gray.

a. Note that if you click somewhere off the table, it will close. To reopen it, double click near the perimeter of the bar graph. If you use the "x" to close the table, double click then right click on the chart and select "datasheet" to reopen.

2. With the table (datasheet) open, right click on the graph and select "chart type." A new window will open allowing you to change the bar graph to a trend line graph. Under "chart type" choose "Line." Under "chart sub-type" choose the first one in the second row. The description of it reads "Line with markers displayed at each data value."

3. Open the table view (if not open). Enter your trend data and predictions into the appropriate cells in the table. The table should look something like this, but with your own data inserted:

	2004	2005	2006	2007e	2008f	2009f	2010f
Historical	136	123	142	126			
Baseline				126	136	122	138

4. With the table still visible, right click on the trend line graph somewhere near the edges of the chart. Select "Chart options." Alternatively, with the table view open, you may select "Chart Options" from the "Chart" heading in the Standard toolbar. A new window will appear with places to change the graph name, axis names and values, data labels, and more.

a. Give the graph an appropriate title and make sure the axes are clearly labeled.

b. Under gridlines, make sure none of the boxes are checked.

c. Under legend, check "bottom."

d. Under data labels, check the box next to "value."

5. Objects within the graph (font size, colors, shape of data points) can be changed by clicking on each object while the table view is open.

    a. Make all the lines and markers black (including foreground and background colors). The past line should be solid. Set the forecast line to short dashes.

    b. All the markers should be set to the diamond shape (in the same window that changed the line colors), with a size of 4 pts.

    c. Delete the background gray color by highlighting (clicking on) the background (called the plot area) and hitting the delete button on your keyboard, or selecting the white color.

    d. Make sure the y-axis is scaled correctly to your data (if it isn't, double click on it and in the new window, and under the "Scale" tab, set the minimum and maximum so that your data takes up most of the graph).

6. Your graph should now look something like Figure 8.4. Note that resizing the object sometimes makes it easier to read.

8.5: Choosing the Benchmarks

You want the benchmark to measure the success of your proposed policy. Choosing benchmarks is not an exact science, but these are guidelines you can follow to make reasonable benchmarks. A benchmark predicts the effectiveness of a policy. The reason you did a baseline is to have something to measure your benchmark against.

The following five guidelines will help you decide.

1. **Pay close attention to the baseline forecast.**

    If the historical trend is steadily getting worse, for example, and the baseline shows the trend continuing, your benchmarks should be conservative. Perhaps holding the line against any more increases might be the best benchmarks. If things look like they have been improving and will continue to improve, your policy should give the trend a big boost in the right direction. If there is no pattern, then a moderate improvement would make sense.

2. **Decide how powerful the factors contributing to the societal problem are.**

    Review the analysis you did in Chapter 5 to examine the causes of the problem. Ask yourself how powerful those causes are and what **your policy** is doing to counteract them.

For example, it may be easier to reduce drunk driving fatalities than to reduce teenage drinking, because everyone wants to reduce drunk driving fatalities, while many teenagers think consuming alcohol is okay. Your estimate of how strong those causes are and how effective your policy will be in curbing those causes will help you decide how ambitious your benchmarks should be.

3. **Estimate how strong government resources are in implementing the policy once the policy has been officially adopted.**

Try to estimate how many government resources will be used to implement the policy. If it involves money, is it enough? Will government enforcement be there if the policy is a new law that might be disobeyed? The nature of the policy also needs to be assessed. For example, policies that call for more education or public relations activities are only going to have a marginal effect in most cases. It is alright to use these policies as long as the impact is not overestimated.

4. **Use comparisons with areas where similar policies have been implemented and base your benchmark on the effectiveness of those policies.**

You can compare conditions from similar geographic areas such as cities or towns and states. The average performance of cities, towns, and villages in a county, for example, can be used as the basis for the benchmark. Comparative data can be used in two ways. The most sensible use of comparative information is to find a locality or state that used your policy and saw some improvement. You can then cite that level of improvement as a basis for your benchmarks. If you cannot find localities that have your policy in place, comparative data is still useful because it can help you to understand how other communities have dealt with your problem and give you some idea of whether or not your benchmarks are reasonable.

The big disadvantage of the comparative approach is that it is time consuming and costly to compile the information. Studying your town compared with five or more other towns requires a lot of time and research. Without the data, you cannot find the average. Getting the data can be difficult because local governments do not necessarily keep good records.

Moreover, the use of comparison assumes that your municipality or state is similar to other municipalities or states used for the comparison. States with a lower per capita income will usually look worse on educational performance compared with those states with richer populations. At the local level, rich communities generally have a lower violent crime rate than poor communities. You also need to take this into account when applying your comparisons.

Despite the dangers, it is always important to consider other areas when developing your benchmark. Professional policy analysts would like to have at least ten similar units to compare, but even three can be helpful. It gives credibility to the benchmark, and it shows that you have thought through your choice carefully.

5. **Select an authoritative source for a benchmark.**

The best approach to choosing and justifying a benchmark is to cite an authoritative government or professional agency. For example, if the Commission on Accreditation of Ambulance Services were to set nine minutes as an acceptable response time for ambulance calls in life-threatening situations in 90 percent of the cases, that standard would become the benchmark to shoot for. Economists usually argue that a 4-6 percent unemployment rate is ideal for the economy. The No Child Left Behind Act sets benchmarks for schools that it considers not to be "failing." In some cases, such benchmarks are not available or they may be too high or too low for the societal conditions you are considering. However, if you can find an authoritative source for a benchmark, you should use it. It means that an official agency has indicated the level of satisfactory performance and the effectiveness of an existing policy.

Case Study

The benchmark selected to determine the success of the Security Awareness Program is that the number of larcenies be 115 by 2010. A drop from 126 in 2007 to 115 in 2010 is expected to result from the heightened awareness of the threat of residence hall robbery when the program kicks off and the fact that the level in 2004 was higher than in the previous year. Given the up and down pattern shown by the percent change calculations, the real test will be if it remains at 115 or below for the next two years. Without the policy, we would expect it to rise as it has in a cyclical fashion in the past. A nearby university with a similar sized undergraduate population in a similar geographical setting has averaged 120 larcenies for the past ten years, which suggests that our benchmark is reasonable.

8.6: Using Benchmarks to Support Your Proposed Policy

Setting a benchmark will help you win support for your policy when presenting it to players. By clearly presenting how you see your policy improving society, you will show that you have thought through the consequences of your policy. You can show what benefits will flow if your policy reaches the benchmark. The main benefit will, of course, be the reduction in your societal problem. Additional benefits are those you considered in Chapter 7. For example, additional benefits could include staff time and monetary costs saved by a policy that reaches its benchmarks. It is not always possible to be exact about these benefits. It is not always possible to be exact about the staff time and monetary costs saved by a policy that reaches its benchmarks. However, even attempting to estimate the benefits will increase the persuasiveness of your case to powerful players.

Benchmarks can help convince key players that a change is needed which is the first step to gaining support for the policy you proposed. You can use benchmarks to help you effectively speak to powerful people in the organization affected by the problem you have identified. Float the benchmarks by these powerful people to test the waters of the organization, and use the results to determine whether to step up your efforts or go back to the drawing board.

Benchmarks should be viewed as a rhetorical device to drive home a point, just as politicians use 30-second sound bites and photo opportunities to gain support. For example, you could convince a state health department to provide prenatal care to your community by showing that its infant mortality rate is not as good as the averages of similar states.

Case Study

In our Citrus University example, you can estimate how much staff time is used on average for each theft. If your policy reduces the number of thefts by 20, for example, and it takes the staff members five hours to investigate each crime, you will save 100 man hours. This will show how beneficial your policy will be. A proponent of the program could argue that the college administration should invest in the program, because if the benchmark is reached, it will show substantial progress and make the college more competitive with other colleges. The trend line graph on the next page compares a baseline forecast with the benchmarks so you can see how much the policy will reduce the number of larcenies.

To insert this graph, follow the instructions in 8.4(a). Instead of making the 3rd row disappear, label it "Benchmark." Your table should look like the following, but with your data.

	2004	2005	2006	2007e	2008f	2009f	2010f
Historical	136	123	142	126			
Baseline				126	136	122	138
Benchmark				126	126	120	115

When you are formatting the lines, make your benchmark line the long dashes line. The graph should end up looking like Figure 8.5.

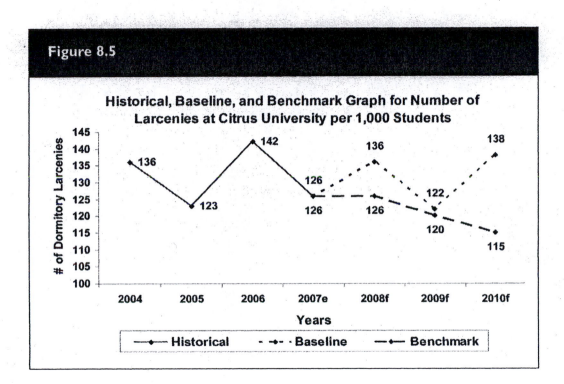

Figure 8.5

Historical, Baseline, and Benchmark Graph for Number of Larcenies at Citrus University per 1,000 Students

Profile of a Maniac Policy Evaluator

Drew Bland

As a senior in the Policy Studies major at Syracuse University, Drew Bland got a position as head of a research team to study the impact of 45 million dollars of federal money given to the City of Syracuse to improve neighborhoods that had fallen on hard times. He organized thousands of records of houses, properties, and business establishments to see if the impact of the money could be traced. His study built on his skills in Microsoft Excel and statistics and was considered remarkable by local officials. He worked with me, government officials, and community people to obtain and analyze the information. His work was considered outstanding for an undergraduate. It will help him get a job and get into a first rate graduate program, and it will help improve many of the neighborhoods in the City of Syracuse. Evaluation usually leads to more money and reaching critical benchmarks.

Chapter 9

Forecasting Implementation with the Prince System

"We cannot insure success, but we can deserve it." — John Adams

YOUR GOAL   To forecast the chances that a policy will be implemented.

Introduction

Good public policy ideas do not become policies without sufficient political support. A method for forecasting the chances that a policy will be implemented is the **Prince System**.

The Prince System, named after Niccolo Machiavelli's book, *The Prince,* is a technique for assessing the relative support or opposition of a public policy decision by various individuals, groups, and organizations.

The Prince System requires the following:

1. Identify the players likely to have a direct or indirect impact on the decision.

2. Determine issue position—whether each player supports, opposes, or is neutral toward the decision.

3. Determine power—how effective each player is in blocking the decision, helping to make it happen, or otherwise affecting the implementation of a decision.

4. Determine priority—how important the decision is to each player.

5. Calculate the likelihood that the policy will be implemented.

You will learn how to perform each of these steps in this chapter. They are demonstrated by case studies.

Describing the Policy to Be Implemented

Begin by clearly describing the public policy you wish to see implemented. Using your preferred alternative developed in Chapters 6, 7, and 8, obtain information on the following:

1. The level of government at which the policy will be implemented: Is it local, state, or federal?

2. Legislative requirements: Does the policy require a new or revised law?

3. Executive/Administrative requirements: What agency will be primarily responsible?

4. Financial requirements: What funds, if any, are required?

5. Judicial decisions: How will the courts affect the policy? What cases could be brought to court resulting from the policy?

Be sure that you have defined a policy and not a goal. For example, "reducing unemployment" is a goal; "Spending $10 million of federal funds to provide job-training programs" is a policy.

Although the policy needs to be clearly described in order to forecast its implementation, the exact details of its final formulation are not required. Frequently, policies are altered to gain the support needed for their approval. For instance, tax plans often begin with tax rates lower than those that eventually appear in the final version.

The following case study provides the description of a policy to deal with the problem of drug abuse in the community of Riverdale.

Case Study

The Riverdale Youth Bureau should create a court with teenagers as judges to try to sentence youths eighteen and under accused of buying, selling, and using drugs. The Teen Court would sentence the offenders to rehabilitation, community service, and serving time on the Teen Court. This program will be controlled by the County Youth Bureau.

New legislation is not needed for implementation of the policy, and all administrative duties will be performed by the program director.

The court will be administered by a new staff person whose salary, expenses, and administrative costs will total $56,000.

No formal court action is required, but the District Attorney and the Town Justice would have to agree to allow this court to operate informally.

Identifying the Players

Reasons for including a player are any of the following:

- The player has substantial legal authority.

- The player has political influence to promote or obstruct the decision. Players that can prevent the policy from being implemented are veto players.

- The player has formal or informal influence on a veto player.

Identifying the players to be considered is one of the most important steps in the Prince System. Including unimportant players or omitting important players can distort the analysis to the extent that it becomes useless.

A key to identifying the correct players is to consider the legislative, administrative, and judicial requirements of the policy. If the proposed policy involves monetary decisions, include players that have authority over the budget. If the proposed policy requires new or revised legislation, include the chief executive and the legislature. If the policy requires neither new funds nor new legislation, include the bureaucracies responsible for the policy and those that influence those bureaucracies. In addition to government officials in the executive and legislative branch, include players representing key interest groups.

To develop your list of players, begin by writing down all those that you think have some degree of influence on the policy, Next, reduce the list to between five and ten of those that you feel are essential.

The principal way to limit the number of players is to group individuals and organizations into collective players for the purpose of analysis. The process of grouping frequently appears arbitrary and can seriously affect the results if it is not done carefully. Guidelines that assist in grouping players to improve the accuracy of the analysis include the following:

■ Group players having the same economic interests. In dealing with an environmental issue, for example, all private developers might be grouped together.

■ Do not group players with veto power. This especially holds for governmental players. For example, for federal policy, never group the President and Congress.

■ Do not group players if there is a disagreement among them or if their components have widely unequal power. For example, members of a city government could be combined as a single player if there were general agreement among them concerning the issue and if each person in the governing unit had approximately equal power. If there were disagreements, or if some members were much more powerful than others, it would be preferable to divide them into two (or more) players.

■ Select a list of players that represents a reasonable picture of the overall power distribution. Do not include an excess of players that give one side unrealistic weight. If there is one collective player with an immense amount of power, that player should be divided into enough smaller players so that the total power is accurately reflected. For example, in dealing with the legislative branch, you might want to list the House of Representatives and the Senate as separate players rather than treat the Congress as a single player.

These guidelines are intentionally quite general. Your judgment in conducting the analysis is vital at every step. Rely on the Prince System as a way of organizing and guiding your analysis. Your success depends on becoming knowledgeable enough to select the right group of players.

In this case study, players are selected for the proposed Riverdale Teen Court:

Case Study

1. James French, District Attorney of Riverdale
   His consent, with that of the judge, is necessary to create the court.

2. Joyce Zeno, County Youth Bureau
   She is responsible for approving youth related programs in the county.

3. K. Westcott, Deputy Director for Local Services in Division for Youth
   She has the authority to allocate funds for youth programs in the state.

4. J. McGrath, Chief of Riverdale Police
   The Chief would have to cooperate with the District Attorney and the Town Justice for the program to operate effectively.

5. Johanna Horton, Town Justice
   Her consent, along with that of the District Attorney, is necessary to create the court.

Estimating Issue Position, Power, and Priority for Each Player

Issue Position is the current attitude of the player toward the policy. It is expressed as a number ranging from +5 to -5 to indicate levels of support or opposition. Assign +5 if the player is firmly in favor of the issue and is unlikely to change; a +4, +3, +2, or +1 indicate lower levels of firmness of the player's support; a neutral position is expressed as 0. Similarly, a -5 indicates firm opposition; a -4, -3, -2, or -1 indicate lower degrees of opposition. When estimating a player's issue position:

- Read and listen to what the player says about the issue.

- Estimate from the player's economic, social, or political standing what the player's position is likely to be on the basis of self-interest.

- Look for differences among individuals and factions within groups and organizations. Look for inconsistencies in statements by individual members. If the contrasting positions seem evenly balanced, assign a 0 (neutral) issue position. If there seems a slight positive or negative balance toward the issue, assign a +1 or -1 for the player's issue position.

Power is defined as the degree to which the player, relative to the other players, can directly or indirectly exert influence concerning the decision of policy implementation. A player's power is based on such factors as group size, wealth, physical resources, institutional authority, prestige, and political skill. Power is expressed as a number ranging from 1 to 5. Assign 1 if the player has a slight amount of power; a 2 if the player has more than minimum power; a 3 or 4 if the player has substantial power; or a 5 if the player can veto or prevent the implementation of the policy with little or no interference by other players. When estimating a player's power:

- Ask if the player has the ability either to block or implement the policy.

- Determine if legal authority is a consideration.

- Consider whether a player has the ability to help or hinder the policy-making process.

- Determine, if need be, the player's wealth.

- Do not assume that a player, powerful on one set of issues, is necessarily powerful on all issues.

- Consider the allies and enemies of the player. Powerful allies increase power; powerful enemies diminish it.

Priority is defined as the importance that the player attaches to supporting or opposing the decision relative to all other decisions with which that player is concerned. Priority is expressed as a number ranging from 1 to 5. Assign 1 to indicate slight interest or concern for the issue regardless of the player's issue position and power. Assign 2 for those players with some concern, while a 3 and 4 indicate substantial concern. A 5 is reserved for those players that give their highest priority to the issue. When estimating priority:

- Determine the frequency and intensity with which the player makes public statements about the issue.

- From the player's social, political, and economic interest, determine the importance the player is likely to attach to the decision.

- Watch out for the fact that priority can be rapidly and substantially altered by external events and the intrusion of other issues.

- Remember that other issues and factors compete for the player's attention and, hence, priority.

As with selecting players, the assignment of issue position, power, and priority requires good information and a solid understanding of the financial, administrative, legislative, and judicial factors affecting the policy. Systematic research can play an important role, but skillful assessment of existing conditions by knowledgeable and sensible observers is absolutely essential. Therefore, you have to be thoroughly familiar with the situation to provide accurate estimates on issue position, power, and priority. You should talk to other knowledgeable people and gather all available information on the reactions of individuals, groups, and organizations to the proposed policy. Refer to Chapters 2, 3, and 4 for a review of information-gathering skills.

Following are the estimates and justifications for the issue position, power, and priority for five players involved in the proposed Riverdale Teen Court:

Case Study

Player One   **James French**

Issue: +1   He feels that the Teen Court may be worth a try, but he fears that high school students may not be morally developed enough to make these decisions about other teens.

Power: 5   His power is high because, as District Attorney, he has veto power, and his consent, with that of the judge, is necessary to create the court.

Priority: 1   His concern is with prosecuting all people who break the law without partiality to any particular offenders. This proposal relates to only a small part of his responsibilities.

Player Two   **Joyce Zeno**

Issue: +4   She believes the Teen Court would be a refreshing new way to attack the drug problem.

Power: 5   She has a lot of power because she could veto the program if she opposed it. Besides, she is director of the bureau that would implement the program.

Priority: 3   She gives the issue high priority because the decision, one way or another, will seriously affect her work. She recently wrote a letter to the editor of the newspaper expressing the need for community concern on the issue.

Player Three   **K. Westcott**

Issue: -2   She opposes the proposal because she favors the traditional court system that can impose stiffer penalties.

Power: 5   Her power is high because she allocates the funds for youth programs in New York State and can veto the project by withholding money.

Priority: 1   Her priority is low because the Teen Court is only one of the many youth programs in the state with which she deals.

Player Four   J. McGrath

Issue: -4   He opposes the program because he feels many teens will see this as just a way to avoid a jail sentence.

Power: 3   As police chief, McGrath has authority and influence in local government and the community and can indirectly affect the implementation of the Teen Court.

Priority: 3   He is concerned about the drug issue but has many other criminal issues with which to deal on his job.

Player Five   Johanna Horton

Issue: 0   Her issue position is neutral because she thinks that the penalties might not be stiff enough, but she does acknowledge that teen courts have been successful in other communities.

Power: 5   The implementation of the program depends on her cooperation as she has final jurisdiction over the offenders, giving her veto power.

Priority: 3   She gives moderate priority to the drug issue but also is concerned with other crimes.

Completing the Prince Chart and Calculating the Probability of the Policy being Accepted

After making estimates of issue position, power, and priority for each player, you can determine the probability that the policy will be implemented. The steps for estimating this probability are illustrated in the following case study, based on a proposed policy for the implementation of a Riverdale Teen Court.

Case Study

Calculation 1: Issue Position x Power x Priority = Prince Score

Multiply issue position, power, and priority for each player to determine the player's Prince Score. For example, James French in Figure 9.1 has an issue position of +1, a power of 5, and a priority of 1. The product of these three numbers is +5. If the issue position is 0, multiply just the power and priority to determine the player's Prince Score, and put a parenthesis around the score. For example, Johanna Horton has a 0 issue position, a power of 5, and priority of 3, leading to a Prince Score of (15). Make sure that you do not forget the negative signs, where appropriate.

POLICY: Implement a Teen Court in Riverdale

(State in terms of **Desired Political Outcome**)

PLAYERS	ISSUE POSITION	X	POWER	X	PRIORITY	=	PRINCE SCORE
James French	+1	X	5	X	1	=	+5
Joyce Zeno	+4	X	5	X	3	=	+60
K. Westcott	-2	X	5	X	1	=	-10
J. McGrath	-4	X	3	X	3	=	-36
Johanna Horton	0	X	5	X	3	=	(15)

CALCULATION OF PROBABILITY:

Calculation 2: Sum of all positive scores plus 1/2 neutral scores = 72.5

Calculation 3: Sum of all scores ignoring signs and parentheses = 126

Calculation 4: Probability of support = Calculation 2 / Calculation 3 = $\frac{72.5}{126}$ = .575 = 58%

Calculation 2: Sum of All Positive Scores Plus 1/2 Neutral Scores

Find the sum of all positive Prince Scores plus 1 /2 the sum of all Prince Scores that are enclosed in parentheses (the neutral scores). In this case, the sum of all positive Prince Scores is 65 (James French is +5 and Joyce Zeno is +60). The neutral score is 15 for the Board of Trustees. Add 1/2 of 15 to the 65 for a total of 72.5 for this calculation.

Calculation 3: Sum of All Scores Ignoring Signs and Parentheses

Find the sum of all Prince Scores ignoring signs and parentheses. In this case, the sum of all scores is 126 (James French is 5, Joyce Zeno is 60, K. Westcott is 10, J. McGrath is 36, and Johanna Horton is 15).

Figure 9.2: Interpretation of Probability

100%	. Certain to be implemented. In the case of 100% agreement on a policy, there is no public policy issue.
60% - 99%	Likely to be implemented
40% - 59%	Uncertain. Likely to be disputed without resolution.
1% - 39%	Unlikely to be implemented. Likely to be killed as a proposal.
0%	Never will be implemented. In case of 0% support of a proposal, there is no public policy issue.

Calculation 4: Probability of Support = Calculation 2 / Calculation 3

Divide the number you found in Calculation 2 by the number you found in Calculation 3. In this case, it would be 72.5 divided by 126 which equals .575 or 58%. The calculation of the probability for the policy analyzed in the Prince Chart in Figure 9.1 indicates that there is a 58% chance that the teen court will be implemented. This indicates that it is uncertain whether the policy will be implemented. See Figure 9.2 for a guide to interpreting such probabilities.

Forecasting Policy Implementation in the News Media

The news media almost never make forecasts concerning whether or not a policy will be implemented. Occasionally, players and experts are asked to make forecasts that are then published. The news media will report which players are supporting proposed policies, but the most powerful players usually have issue positions that are not firm. These players will take pains to keep their options open or, if they have reached a decision, not to make their views public. As a result, it is difficult to get clear information on the issue position, power, and priority of players as well as on the general likelihood of a policy proposal from the media.

Profile of Policy-Makers

Shane Bucher,
Anthony Chiaravalloti,
Eric Friedman and
Michael Woodward

When these four seniors at East Syracuse-Minoa High School discovered that recycling in the district had dropped by one-third in the last five years, they decided to do something about it. To them, it became more than modules in PAF 101; it was about doing something for the environment. Based on the students' suggestions at a Board of Education meeting, the district wrote its first recycling policy. To increase recycling, the boys recommended and implemented a three-bin system. Using this system, the students projected that the district would produce five tons of recycled material by the 2008-2009 school year, bringing recycling back to its 2002 level. By lining up the Superintendent and the School Board, as well as the janitors and the student government, these four students created a new policy that will benefit the district and the community for many years to come.

Chapter 10

Developing Political Strategies

"There is nothing more difficult to carry out, nor more doubtful of success, nor more dangerous to handle, than to initiate a new order of things."

— Niccolo Machiavelli

> **YOUR GOAL**   To develop strategies for affecting the chances that a policy will be implemented.

Introduction

In Chapter 9, you learned how to forecast the likelihood that a proposed policy would be implemented. That analysis is based on the information you have about political support and opposition at a given time. However, political support and opposition can change constantly as a result of elections, new social conditions, or even accidents. For example, the support for large government expenditures on drug education may suddenly increase when an athlete, actor, or other well-known figure dies from a drug overdose.

Among the main sources of change are the actions different players take to support or oppose a policy. For example, Mothers Against Drunk Driving (MADD) often threatens to oppose legislators seeking re-election if they do not vote for strong DWI laws. These actions are called strategies because they are taken to achieve a specific goal: to increase or decrease the likelihood that a policy will be implemented.

In this chapter, you will learn how to formulate a strategy using the information you gathered in Chapter 9. The case studies that began in Chapter 9 will be extended into this chapter.

Selecting a Player for Developing a Strategy

The first step in developing a strategy is to determine whether or not you want a policy implemented or defeated. You can make a decision on the basis of your own feelings about the policy or select a position based on other considerations.

The exercises in this chapter require you to develop a strategy on behalf of one of the players in your Prince analysis from Chapter 9. Select a player that has a firm issue position and high priority. Do not select a player unless that player has a score of at least 3 on both factors. The reason for this is that players with scores of less than a 3 on issue position and priority are not likely to pursue a strategy since they are open to changing their position and do not care enough to take strong action. Your selection of a player may also depend upon your knowledge of the player's power. Select a player with a significant amount of power, because such a player will have more strategies available.

The following case study shows an example of player selection for the proposed policy discussed in Chapter 9.

Case Study

For the proposed Riverdale Teen Court, the player chosen is Ms. Joyce Zeno. There are many reasons to choose Ms. Zeno: Ms. Zeno has a lot of power (5) in her position as Director of the Youth Bureau. Thus, she can choose from a wide variety of strategies. Her issue position is a +4, which means she has a firm position in support of the policy. She also gives the Teen Court policy a moderate priority (3), so she will be willing to work hard to change the positions of others to increase support for the Teen Court.

Describing a Political Strategy

You are now ready to select specific actions to increase the support for your player's position on the issue. Your goal is to take actions that change the positions of other players so the situation becomes more favorable to you.

- If your goal is to increase the chances that the policy will be implemented, develop a strategy to increase the issue position and priority of other players, especially those with high power.

- If your goal is to reduce the chances that the policy will be implemented, develop a strategy to decrease the issue position and increase the priority of other players, especially those with high power.

- For players that have a firm position opposite to yours, develop a strategy to decrease their issue position.

Your strategy need not cause a complete shift; any movement toward your goal is an improvement. Four basic strategies for achieving your goal are:

1. Add new players that have the issue position, priority, and power that you want, or delete players that are undesirable from your point of view.

2. Change the issue position of players.

3. Change the power of players.

4. Change the priority of players.

In planning your strategic action, it is important to distinguish between strategy goals and the strategies to achieve these goals. Strategy goals include various desired changes that would alter probability as you wish it to be altered. Strategies are the specific actions you decide to take to achieve your goals. For example, a goal might be to raise players' priorities. The strategy to achieve that goal might be to issue a statement to the news media that will raise the players' priority levels.

Strategies for Achieving Strategy Goals

1. *Add new players or delete existing players.*

    This strategy goal can radically alter the chances of a decision, but it is very difficult to implement. For any public policy issue, players in the game are not likely to leave. The exceptions are politicians who lose elections and individuals with health or personal problems. New players might be added as a result of elections, and campaigning actively for certain candidates would be one way to achieve that strategy goal. Adding new players can also be accomplished by creating new organizations. For example, various students who support a particular school policy change could establish a formal organization as a strategy.

2. *Change the issue position of players.*

    This strategy goal is the most frequently sought. Its effectiveness depends on the power and skill of the player using it and the attitudes of the target players. There are four basic ways to change a player's issue position:

    ■   Make specific promises to do something in exchange for a shift in issue position. In legislatures, this is called logrolling; when one legislator supports one bill in order to win another legislator's support on another issue. Campaign contributors promise money in exchange for support promised by candidates. This often works best when you work with special interest groups on a strategy.

- Redefine the policy to accommodate the interests of those opposed without sacrificing its essential ingredients. This is usually called compromise; it is found in all kinds of decision-making political bodies.

- Make threats to do something unpleasant if the player does not shift position. Lobbyists and legislators sometimes resort to threats if promises do not work.

- Make arguments that use facts and emotional appeals to change the player's mind. This is a form of lobbying. This strategy is always necessary, but it cannot be used by itself. It must be accompanied by other strategies in order to work.

The four ways to change issue positions of players are listed in the order of general effectiveness. Promises and compromise are less costly than threats to the player pursuing the strategy. Threats are costly because they can backfire. The player might stick to its own position even more firmly. Threats, therefore, should be used only as a last resort. Arguments are made by all players all the time; as a result, they have limited effectiveness. Although arguments are a necessary ingredient to any strategy, they never work by themselves.

The firmer a player's issue position, the more difficult it is to move that player. If the player is on your side, a firm position indicates a reliable ally. If the player is on the opposite side, firmness is a measure of how difficult it will be to get your strategy to work. If you move a player that is -5 to a +1, the chances of success are increased more than if you move a -1 player to a +1. However, it is easier to move the -1 player to a +1. You often have to choose between a large chance of a small gain against a small chance of a large gain.

3. *Change the power of yourself and other players.*

   Power comes from a variety of sources, including:

   - Appointed or elected position in the policy-making process

   - Wealth

   - Organizational size and cohesion

   - Reputation for knowledge

   - Number and importance of friends and enemies

Increasing the power of your allies and decreasing the power of your opponents takes a long time and a great deal of work. However, there may be no other choice.

Remember, you obtain maximum results from power strategies if you direct them at players with firm positions and high priorities.

4. *Change the priority of other players.*

Priority strategies fall into three categories:

- Trying to raise priority by creating events that generate publicity or distributing information on the issue. Issuing a news release or writing a public service announcement are ways to do this.

- Trying to lower priority by keeping the issue quiet or generating other issues that take your issue out of the spotlight.

- Trying to raise or lower priority by compromising or redefining a proposed policy.

Use publicity with care. It is not always to your advantage to raise the priority of all players. If your opponents have high priority and those who support you have lower priority, raising priority will improve your situation. However, if your supporters already have high priority and your opponents do not, raising priority will hurt you. In fact, in this case, your strategy goal should be to lower priority among players.

To formulate an effective political strategy, once you have decided on the player you wish to represent, do the following:

- Decide on which players you wish to concentrate.

- Consider the four types of strategy goals just presented.

- Select a strategy that will move players in the direction you want.

Make sure that the player you represent can actually carry out the strategy. Spell out the specific steps that might be taken to execute your strategy. Some examples of specific steps that you could take are lobbying or issuing press releases.
The following case study explores an example of a strategy:

Case Study

For the proposed Riverdale Teen Court, Joyce Zeno will try to decrease opposition to the policy by using the strategy of compromise. She recognizes James French's concern that teens may not be morally developed enough to make such mature decisions. She will propose creating an advisory board to review the decisions made by the court. This board would consist of herself, Mr. French, and members of the community who are interested in and knowledgeable about the issue.

Assessing the Impact of the Proposed Strategy

Once you have described your strategy, discuss its impact. Forecast how each of the players will be affected by the strategies. Examine the effects of your strategy on each player even if the strategy is designed to work primarily on only one. Remember that the players are constantly keeping track of one another; there will be some indirect effects of any strategy you pursue.

To assess the impact of your strategy:

1. Provide a summary of what changes you expect in issue position, power, and priority as a result of your strategy.

2. Recalculate a new Prince Chart with the changed issue position, power, and priority scores.

Remember also that different strategies have different effects on different players. Promises, compromises, threats, and arguments will change only the issue position of players. Increasing publicity through such actions as petitions, pickets, and demonstrations will raise priority, but may not change either issue position or power. Most power strategies take a long time to be effective and may affect several players.

The following describes the impact of the strategy proposed in the Case Study on page 121 on the players involved with the proposed Riverdale Teen Court. An "S" indicates that the score remained the same.

Case Study

Player	Original Score		New Score	Reasons
James French	Position	+1	+3	His main reservation was the possibility that teens might
	Power	5	S	not make responsible decisions. If there is an adult board,
	Priority	1	S	he is willing to give the policy more of a chance.
K. Westcott	Position	-2	S	The compromise does not change her opposition. She
	Power	5	S	still favors the traditional court system.
	Priority	1	S	
J. McGrath	Position	-4	-2	He was afraid the teens would just see the Teen Court
	Power	3	S	as a way to avoid a jail sentence. His opposition to the
	Priority	3	S	proposal is less as he thinks an advisory board may be
				able to monitor this, although he still has reservations.
Johanna Horton	Position	0	+1	She feels that the board could monitor the penalties and
	Power	5	S	make sure they are stiff enough. Thus, she gives slight sup-
	Priority	3	2	port to the policy. Her priority declines because she is
				no longer concerned about negative effects of the policy.

The following shows the new Prince Chart based on the results of the strategy:

Players	Issue Position	X	Power	X	Priority	=	Player's Prince Score
	-5 to +5		1 to 5		1 to 5		
James French	+3	X	5	X	1	=	+15
Joyce Zeno	+4	X	5	X	3	=	+60
K. Westcott	-2	X	5	X	1	=	-10
J. McGrath	-2	X	3	X	3	=	-18
Johanna Horton	+1	X	5	X	2	=	+10

Calculation of Probability

Calculation 2:   Sum of all positive scores plus 1/2 neutral scores = 85

Calculation 3:   Sum of all scores ignoring signs and parentheses = 113

Calculation 4:   Probability = Calculation 2/Calculation 3

$$= \frac{85}{113} = .75 = 75\%$$

Discussing Strategies for Policy Implementation from the News Media

The strategies considered by players to deal with a proposed policy are rarely described in the news media because timing and surprise are often key ingredients. An occasional source of this information is the news analysis television or radio programs where observers are asked to speculate on the strategies that might be followed by a given player. Another source would be the strategies followed by interest groups that adopt a public stance on an issue.

Profile of a Public Policy Analyst for Business

Melvin Norris

Melvin Norris graduated from Syracuse University in 1995 and went to work with Congressman Charles Rangel. After several years in this position, Melvin became the Deputy Director of Public Policy and Government Affairs for Verizon. He is responsible for maintaining relationships with local (New York City) and elected state officials, and lobbying on behalf of the company. He also does community affairs work making sure that nonprofit institutions and cultural institutions receive financial backing from Verizon. Here is what he said when he wrote asking for help:

"I am writing to you because I need your help. This is straight from PAF 101 when you have to identify the players you need in order to institute a policy (I tell you the things you taught me never leave). Verizon is undergoing a national initiative to get into the cable business. Right now, the cable industry in New York State is a monopoly. The way it is set up, each locality has one cable provider and the customers are stuck with that provider if they want cable service. Complaints range from price to service quality. With another cable provider entering the market, it benefits customers since it lowers prices (I have studies that prove this) and improves service quality for fear of customers leaving their service for another provider."

Melvin was looking for faculty to write newspaper opinion pieces and position papers.

Chapter 11

Preparing a Policy Memo
and Briefing Paper

"I would have written a shorter letter, but I didn't have the time."
— Blaise Pascal

YOUR GOAL   To create a clear, concise, and sound policy proposal in two different formats based on the concepts presented in Chapters 1-10.

Introduction

This chapter provides guidelines for writing a Policy Memo which is usually no more than 300 words and a Briefing Paper which can run up to 2,000 words. Either format can be used to integrate the work you have completed in Chapters 1-10. Each is described below with specific guidelines.

Policy Memo

A Policy Memo is usually written by senior staff members to help their boss, a politician, or the head of an agency quickly review an idea that might become a public policy initiative. It has to be short and to the point because the staff member's boss cannot waste time. Each office may have a different format, but they all answer these four questions:

1.   What problem does the policy address? Use about 75 words to specifically identify the societal problem, its most important negative consequences, and the primary causes. (Covered in Chapter 5)

2. What is the proposed policy? Use about 75 words to clearly describe the government action you are suggesting. Try to estimate the cost if you can. (Covered in Chapter 6)

3. What benchmarks will you use to see if the policy is successful? Use about 75 words to indicate the three years in which your benchmarks will be measured, and give actual statistics that you hope to see if your benchmarks are successful. Suggest the most important reason why you think the benchmarks will be reached. (Covered in Chapter 8)

4. What is the political feasibility of your proposal? State the feasibility (high, medium, or low). Use about 75 words to identify the most important groups of players that would support or oppose the proposed policy. Be sure to suggest the reason for their opposition and also to make a forecast. (Covered in Chapter 9, but don't use the terminology of the Prince Chart)

Staff members usually try to keep the memo to 300 words because their bosses like one page. You can do this if you get to the point and precisely answer the questions. Failure to meet the word limit suggests that your writing is too wordy, in which case you should read a book written more than 75 years ago, *The Elements of Style* by William Strunk, Jr. and E.B. White. Failure to meet the word limit could also mean that you have not organized your ideas well enough, which means you need to make a very careful outline.

Public Policy Briefing Paper

A Policy Briefing paper is not written for internal staff purposes; it is written to leaders of government and nonprofit organizations and elected officials who you feel could benefit from your research and ideas. It should be no more than 2,000 words. The format presented in this chapter is widely used by top leaders in business, government, and the non-profit sector.

Start the paper with a one-page **executive summary** that describes each of the other sections of the paper. Then write a **formulation** section that clearly identifies the problem and the causes contributing to the problem. The next section, **implementation**, discusses what needs to be done to implement the policy both administratively and politically. The final section, **evaluation**, discusses your plans for evaluating the policy after it has been implemented.

The guidelines presented on the next few pages can be used without having done the exercises in Chapters 1-10, but if you have done those exercises, your first step is to review your work, particularly in Chapters 5-10.

In the five previous chapters, you completed a series of steps that began with identifying a societal problem, proposing a public policy to deal with that problem, forecasting the impact of that policy, and analyzing the chances of the policy being implemented. The critical stage in the analysis was the selection of the policy alternative.

In selecting the policy in Module 3, you were asked to weigh the effectiveness and political feasibility of your proposed policy against the effectiveness and political feasibility of alternative policies. Because you had not conducted the analysis required in Chapters 7, 8, 9, and 10 prior to Module 3, your initial judgment was not as informed as it is now.

As a result of your additional knowledge and analysis, you should now reach one of the following conclusions:

1. Your policy as stated was the best among the alternatives you suggested.

2. Your policy was on the right track, but it needs revision because of uncertainty about its benefits and costs (covered in Chapter 7) or because of questions about its political feasibility (covered in Chapters 9 and 10).

3. One of the other policy alternatives considered in Chapter 6 would be better than the one you have been analyzing.

4. A completely new alternative would be preferable.

Once you have reviewed your previous work, you are ready to write each of the four sections described below. In writing the paper, keep in mind for your audience at least one specific player in order to decide how much detail and background to include. The player should be an official in the administration, the legislature, or a lobbying group. Although your paper may also be addressed to broader audiences, such as readers of the newspaper or influential members of the community, keep at least one specific player in mind when drafting your paper.

EXECUTIVE SUMMARY

The purpose of the executive summary is to give the reader an idea of what is contained in the paper. Although it is the first section of the paper, it should be written last, using material from the rest of the paper. The executive summary should follow the organization of the paper exactly. In fact, some of the same sentences that appear in the executive summary may be used to introduce each section of the paper. The executive summary should be comprehensive enough to be understood without reading the remainder of the report.

(Suggested length: 300 words)

FORMULATION

The formulation section should do the following:

1. Identify a societal problem you seek to alleviate through your policy. Provide evidence that demonstrates the extent of the problem.

2. Discuss the social, economic, and political factors that contribute to the problem you have identified.

3. Discuss at least three specific public policy proposals that might deal with the problem. Select and justify the one you think will be the most effective and politically feasible. Your policy can require local, state, or federal action by a government agency. All three proposals should be based on action in the same geographical jurisdiction.

(Suggested length: 300 to 600 words)

IMPLEMENTATION

Implementation means putting the public policy into effect. To assess whether a policy will be implemented, answer these questions:

1. What are the financial requirements of the policy? What will be the source of any required funds? Some public policies require very little government spending, while others require a great deal. Although you cannot specify the exact amount of money required, you can give a general estimate. If finances are significant, indicate what government agency will provide the funds.

2. What are the legislative requirements? Some public policies require legislation; others just require an administrative decision. Indicate whether and at which level (local, state, or federal) legislation is required.

3. What are the required administrative operations? "Administrative operations" are activities officials perform on a routine basis. Some policies require such activities; others do not.

4. What are the chances the policy will be implemented? Discuss the degree to which the policy is supported and opposed by players involved in making policy. "Players" are leaders and individuals who will directly or indirectly determine the formulation and actual implementation of the policy. They include those formally responsible for making policy, those who influence policy makers, and those who will be able to affect the way the policy is implemented. Assess the relative strengths of the supporting and

opposing forces to forecast the likelihood that the policy will be maintained or implemented.

The implementation section of the paper will demonstrate your understanding of the political realities surrounding public policy decisions. It is not enough to identify a good public policy alternative; you must also assess the chances that the policy will be implemented. Although your analysis will not be completely useless if you choose a policy that has only a small chance of being adopted, failing to recognize the odds against a policy will seriously damage your credibility in the eyes of those who evaluate your arguments. When discussing chances of implementation, indicate under what conditions and strategies the chances might increase or decrease.

(Suggested length: 300 to 600 words)

EVALUATION

The last step in the analysis of a public policy issue is to evaluate whether a public policy has had the desired effect: Has it worked? Since your paper will discuss a policy that has not been put into effect, an actual evaluation cannot be carried out. You can, however, indicate a plan for evaluating the effect of the policy.

To do this, begin by considering the problem you sought to remedy with the policy. Complete a list of the benefits and costs of the policy you advocated. Benefits are the advantages produced by implementing the policy. Costs include the direct expenditures required by the policy and the undesirable consequences that might result directly or indirectly from the policy. Once you have completed this list, discuss how each benefit and cost will be measured. The section must answer:

1. What are the expected benefits of your proposed policy and how will you assess them?

2. What are the expected costs of your proposed policy and how will you assess them?

You will find it difficult to measure benefits and costs, because in some cases, the expected results of a policy are intangible. However, with any public policy issue, even intangible benefits and costs can be measured through surveys of experts or groups affected by the policy.

(Suggested length: 300 words)

Profile of a Policy Staffer

Emily Pecachek

Emily Pecachek was a college freshman when she took my introductory PAF 101 course. She volunteered to help edit and proof opinion pieces I was writing for some newspapers. On her resume, Emily included her experience editing for a Maxwell professor when she applied for a prestigious internship as a freshman on a congressional campaign back in her home state of Minnesota. She got the internship over 50 other students who were juniors and seniors. When the candidate saw how well she wrote, she was hired to become the deputy campaign manager at 19 years old. From that experience, she became a student leader on campus, created a college PAC, and was offered several positions with politicians even before she graduated college. Don't ever underestimate the power of writing precisely and concisely.

Chapter 12

Change Agent Exercises

"First they ignore you, then they laugh at you, then they fight you, then you win."
—Mahatma Gandhi

YOUR GOAL To have a backbone so you can make the world a better place.

Introduction

So now you have all the analytical and writing tools you need to come up with public policies that will make the world better. That doesn't mean a thing unless you can bring about change. This chapter will give you some very specific exercises that will help you conquer your fears of rejection, ignore the apathy of the world around you, and fight for a better community, a better America, and a better world.

This Chapter assumes that you have all the skills covered in Chapters 1-11 and that you have come up with a policy proposal you want to be implemented.

Change agents also need character like the persistence of a John Dau, one of the Lost Boys of Sudan, discussed in the Introduction or Wendy Kopp, Founder of Teach for America, discussed in Chapter 1. Character also means the courage of a Benjamin Franklin or George Washington who challenged the British, Martin Luther King, Jr. who challenged the racists, or Nelson Mandela who led South Africa to a multi-racial regime.

You may not have the same depth of character as these great leaders did, but you may. Challenge yourself by righting wrongs even if it is only getting your roommate to respect differences among people in the residence hall or your professor to keep office hours. Change agents always start small but end up large. You can too. Throughout this chapter, case studies are provided describing an actual organization, called Undergraduates for a Better Education (UBE). Each case study concludes with a set of specific exercises you must complete in order to begin to understand and apply the guidelines provided. Before you read further, here is some background on UBE. It will help you understand the examples in each case study. You can skip them, but you might find them helpful in driving home the point.

UBE STORIES:
History of Undergraduates for a Better Education

UBE was started in the fall of 1986 by a group of seven students who were concerned about problems with their undergraduate education at Syracuse University. The students were members of PAF 101: Introduction to the Analysis of Public Policy. The students wanted to get together to talk about great public policy issues in a voluntary session after class. I agreed to hold the sessions but said to the students: "let's walk, not talk; let's focus on Syracuse University instead of the universe." The students agreed and decided to do something to make SU better for all those affected by its actions. They wanted to transmit Syracuse University to future undergraduates a greater, better, and more beautiful educational experience than they had found it.

In the spring of 1987, the group members designed and conducted a survey of 400 undergraduates and 50 faculty members. Its purpose was to identify student concerns that directly affect undergraduate education. Results indicated that teaching assistants who could not communicate effectively were the number one educational problem at the University. In the fall of 1987, the group used that information to publish a report entitled "Toward the Improvement of Undergraduate Education at Syracuse University." UBE's co-presidents were invited to meet with the dean of the College of Arts and Sciences and the vice president of undergraduate studies to discuss the report.

After that first year of beginning activism, UBE became the leading change agent group on campus dedicated to improving undergraduate education. Numerous articles were written about the group and its work in college, local, and national newspapers. Members were asked to attend panel discussions at every level of the University community, and the group held two national conferences (attendees included the University of Alabama at Birmingham, the University of Illinois at Urbana-Champaign, Case Western Reserve University, and the State University of New York at Binghamton).

Even though undergraduate education has improved greatly at Syracuse University since its birth, UBE continues to be an active change agent. Each activity serves to make learning for Syracuse University undergraduates a little bit better.

This Chapter presents five basic rules that are absolutely essential to success as a change agent. Practice them on your friends and family, and you will be ready to MAKE A DIFFERENCE.

Rule #1: FACE DOWN FEAR

A change agent is someone who is very dissatisfied with the status quo and who has a powerful drive to rescue others, to make right what is wrong, to solve problems, and to never be satisfied. If you choose the change agent path, you have selected the road less traveled. It means you are extraordinary. Therein lies the major obstacle to visualizing yourself as a change agent, because you become the pebble in the shoe, the burr in the saddle, and the bug for everyone else.

Here's an example:
At some point in your life, you probably had to deal with a really incompetent teacher. You sat in a class in which the teacher wrote notes on the blackboard and faced it while lecturing. You could hardly hear what he was mumbling, and you could not even read the notes. If there was ever a reason for you to want to change the status quo, either by getting the teacher to change his behavior or getting him out of the classroom, that was it.

But did you? Or did you instead take care of this irritation by adopting one or more of the following avoidance techniques?

- Coped: Read the book and got an A on the test, so why bother?

- Resigned Yourself: Decided you could do nothing to change the powerful institutions that put this clown in that spot.

- Did a Cost-Benefit Analysis: Avoided taking action for fear of getting a lower grade or being kicked out of school.

- Decided Not to Lose Friends: Excused your willingness to accept the status quo by concluding that your friends were more chicken than you and if you did something, you would be left hanging.

- Toughed it Out: Thought, "Oh well, school sucks and I graduate in a year."

- Acted like a Brat: Showed your displeasure by throwing spitballs at the teacher.

All those responses are typical defense mechanisms designed to let you off the hook. Which one did you use the last time you faced an incompetent teacher, unfair manager at your workplace, or a friend who did something you found unethical?

There are two reasons why everyone, including you, is afraid to become a serious change agent. Fortunately, you can overcome your fear by understanding these reasons and by practicing courage and persistence.

Reason #1: The people in charge could hurt you badly.

Let's say you are in a class where the teacher doesn't give clear assignments and doesn't keep office hours. Why not go to the teacher's boss and lodge a complaint? If you do that, you could end up with a bad grade and a reputation as a trouble-maker. People don't like inflicting pain on themselves, so this is not an unreasonable fear.

Remedy for Reason #1: Rolihlahla or trouble-makers are tough.

Nelson Mandela, in his freshman year of college, stood up to the authorities on a matter of principles and was thrown out of school. We all know about his 27 years in a South African prison. No wonder his father named him Rolihlahla at birth. In his autobiography, *Long Walk to Freedom*, Mandela writes, "in Xhosa, rolihlahla literally means 'pulling the branch of a tree' but its colloquial meaning more accurately would be 'troublemaker'" (p. 3).

Nelson's trouble-making moved South Africa from a very racist and oppressive society closer to the good society. Certainly his pain was worth the world's gain and maybe his own personal satisfaction. Is that why he did it? Or was he merely living up to the role his father visualized for him?

Change agents must come to grips with the realization that they will occasionally be pulling the branch of a tree and that they will be spanked by those in power. They must do what Rolihlahla did and make the necessary sacrifice. No one reading this book is likely to make the magnitude of sacrifice that Nelson Mandela did, but any positive change in life is worthwhile. Visualize yourself as a troublemaker who will be punished, and remember: NO PAIN, NO GAIN.

Reason #2: Your peers will hurt you even worse.

The herd instinct, or what sociologists call "peer group pressure," is so powerful that most people buckle under it most of the time. Fear of being thrown out of the herd is real and ever present. The act of throwing a spitball at the boring teacher suggests that fear of authority is less powerful than fear of the loss of peer approval.

If history is any guide, a strong and sustained stand to promote change for the good society will not be sanctioned by the herd. Herds in democracy generally like leaders who take few risks because they seek to satisfy the special interests of as many as possible. Strong leadership for the public interest threatens the special interests served by the status quo. It increases risks for those who have the most. If you try to fight on a sustained basis for the good of all, you risk the threat of being kicked out of the herd.

Remedy for Reason #2: If your peers told you to stick your head in the toilet, would you?

Excuse the distasteful imagery, but we need to make a powerful point here. If the herd dominated the human race, we would have gone the way of the dinosaurs. Obviously some people left the pack, suffered the consequences, and then had the good fortune to see the pack veering down their path.

If you choose to become a change agent for the public interest, you will be ridiculed by others. You will be called a bleeding heart, troublemaker, naysayer, and mean spirited. You will be told, "You're not a team player," and "Get off your high horse." You will be asked, "Who made you God anyway?" You and your ideas will be ignored. You will suffer losses that may far exceed any personal benefit you may obtain, except the satisfaction of knowing the world is a little better than it would have been.

The bottom line is that if you want to change things at any level, you must sacrifice some of your comforts. Once you recognize this, you are ready to begin to see yourself as a change agent for the good society.

UBE STORIES:
Face Down Fear

At the beginning of the chapter, we defined a change agent as someone who is very dissatisfied with the status quo and who has a powerful drive to rescue others, to make right what is wrong, to solve problems, and to never be satisfied. There is no better way to describe the founding members of UBE. They were upset with the quality of the undergraduate education being provided by Syracuse University. For themselves and the students at SU, they wanted to solve the University's problems and make right what was wrong. This meant they had to become troublemakers.

Will I get kicked out of school? That is a question that has been frequently asked, over the years, by presidents and members of UBE. UBE has pulled quite a few stunts that have angered University officials. Its members constantly worried about what would happen to them for the trouble they were causing. "Will I get kicked out of school?" was a constant topic of conversation. The answer is no, because one of the great strengths of universities is tolerance of different viewpoints. In fact, most administrators were pleasantly surprised to see a group of undergraduates take their education so seriously, and some even liked the pressure the students were exerting. However, even though any sane outside observer would dismiss the concern of UBE members as unnecessary paranoia, this did little good. Fear of punishment by those in charge comes with the change agent role. Sometimes it is warranted, as in the case of Nelson Mandela, and sometimes it is not, as in the case of UBE. In either case, change agents must face down the fear of what the authorities will do to them.

Why do so few students help UBE? You must remember that if you choose the change agent path, you select the road less traveled. It means you are extraordinary. Any person who has ever been a member of UBE will tell you this is true. Of 10,000 undergraduates at Syracuse University, 15 are members of UBE. Most college students aren't about to take on the authorities over the quality of their education. They are busy with athletics, social life, and even soap operas, and they do not want to make more work for themselves. As a result, most fail to participate in UBE's activities because they follow the herd. Fear of separation from the herd deters many UBE joiners, but that fear can be overcome by understanding it. In being a part of UBE, many members find new friends; some, a new herd.

As a change agent, you should realize that you will be fearful and that you must confront that fear. To ignore it produces a variety of behaviors that reduces your effectiveness as a change agent. You will be defensive, openly hostile for no other reason but releasing tension from your fear (like the spitball thrower), and you will lurch, like a manic-depressive, from periods of over-confidence and optimism to periods of despair and hopelessness. None of these ups and downs are helpful. A change agent must be steady inside while at the same time acting in a wide variety of ways toward the rest of the world. This cannot be done unless fear is recognized as part of the game and continually faced down.

Exercise A: Practice Facing Down Fear

Within 24 hours, select a pebble in your shoe from either your own personal life (significant other, friend, or neighbor) or some organization in which you are a stakeholder. Speak to the relevant person about changing his or her behavior and tell somebody else what you did. Then answer the following questions:

1. Were you initially afraid to do it? If so, why?

2. How did the relevant person react to what you said? If you were punished, how terrible was it? If not, why do you think you had fears in the first place? If you are not sure, think about it.

3. Do you think it will be easier the next time you have to initiate a change?

Rule #2: USE DIFFERENT CHANGE AGENT STYLES

If you are ready to be a troublemaker and the leader of a new pack, you need to visualize how you will challenge the authorities and gain support. **Two basic change agent styles are described below. You will use the first most of the time, especially when gaining allies, and the second only when necessary.**

THE DALE CARNEGIE MODEL:
If You Want Honey, Don't Kick Over the Beehive

In *How to Win Friends and Influence People*, one of the best-selling books of all time, author Dale Carnegie suggests that the way to get people to do what you want is to be nice, avoid confrontation, and build positive networks. His principles suggest that once you get into an argument, you have already lost, and that the secret is to get people to come to your way of thinking by thinking it is their way of thinking. Read his book and your ability to work with people will improve 100 percent.

THE SAUL ALINSKY MODEL:
Angry and Proud of It

Saul Alinsky was a 1960s radical who worked to get rights and economic opportunity for the poor. He used such tactics as threatening to get poor folk to eat lots of beans and then attend a classical concert where all the rich people would be. Then those in power would integrate their workforce. He liked shock, hostility, and embarrassment as a way to get what he called the Haves to give some to the Have-nots. To get a better picture of Alinsky's tactics and thinking, and to understand what kind of psychological tool being a change agent takes, read his *Rules for Radicals*. Read this book and see the possibilities of rudeness.

Think of a continuum from Alinsky to Carnegie. For any given situation you might want to change, you must visualize where you want to be on that continuum. This requires both self-analysis and analysis of the situation. Are you someone with a short fuse who likes to let off steam and intimidate people? If so, you would feel comfortable with the Alinsky model. Are you someone who needs to be liked and who avoids confrontation? If so, the Dale Carnegie model is for you.

However, changing something is not just about you, so it's important to choose the proper stance at the proper time and for the proper situation. If you are the angry type, chill out and try a little Carnegie. If you are the peacemaker type, get some backbone and try a little Alinsky. While your basic style is important, you must be flexible and visualize yourself as someone who can turn on the charm or lower the boom.

UBE STORIES:
A Pinch of Alinsky and a Dose of Carnegie

Knowing they needed the support of students and the power of faculty and administrators, UBE members realized they had to choose the proper stance at the proper time. They could not be angry all the time and they could not be peacemakers all the time. They had to find a happy medium between the Alinsky model and the Carnegie model. Understanding this concept, UBE's activities have used a mixture of both styles. Some are meant to get the attention of the faculty and administration by really angering students and parents. Others have helped improve undergraduate education by building strong relationships between UBE and the administration.

Here are examples of each:

UBE and "Alinsky": There is probably nothing that will make the administration of a university change its habits faster then angry parents—especially angry parents who are spending over $40,000 a year to send their children to school. UBE members knew that when they distributed flyers during an annual Parents Weekend celebration. The flyers given out to parents were entitled, "Are You Getting What You Pay For?" and described several problems with undergraduate education at SU. This was an effort to do two things: 1) anger parents into forcing the administration to make changes, and 2) scare the administration into making changes by worrying them that if parents were angry enough they would pull their kids from the school.

UBE and "Carnegie": Dale Carnegie thought it was important to build positive networks. In many cases, UBE members agree, which is why so many of them sit on various University committees. One of the group's goals is to serve as a resource for faculty, administrators, and staff when they seek student opinions about academic issues. So when a committee is looking for student input, they often come to UBE.

It is always better to be in the Dale Carnegie mode, but frequently you have to use a little Alinsky to "train" those in charge.

Each year, Syracuse University has a guest speaker speak to members of the freshman class. The speaker is supposed to build relationships between the first-year students by stimulating intellectual conversation among them. The speaker in 1997, the first year of the program, was a natural science professor from Harvard University who gave a very poorly received talk, apparently enjoyed by only a few natural science undergraduates and those professors who specialized in his field—certainly not the vast majority of freshmen. After the lecture, one UBE member started asking questions, trying to find out who chose the speaker and if any students had been involved in the decision. Sure enough, it was a group of Arts and Sciences faculty members and administrators. Not a single student had a voice in the decision.

The UBE member knew something had to be done about that, so she decided to introduce herself to the dean in charge of the committee. Without bringing up how terrible she thought the lecturer had been, she asked the dean if he would mind if a student sat on the committee to help choose the next year's lecturer. He told her that he would think about it, but that he felt he was very "paternal" and could make that decision without student input. She knew at that point that new measures had to be taken or a student would never sit on the freshman lecture committee.

Here is where Alinsky measures came into play. The UBE member conducted a quick written survey of freshmen who had attended the lecture. The survey results showed uniform negative opinions and was presented to the entire freshman lecture committee. A few days later, the committee asked her to be a student representative to the committee. Two years later she still had a voice in who speaks to the freshmen each year.

In short, your "best practice" is to use a variety of styles at your command and to act out those styles as the situation dictates. Be aware that you may have to change style in a matter of seconds. You can act like Alinsky in private with your supporters by making all kinds of macho, out-of-control statements about what you are going to do to those in authority. Then you may go into a meeting and act sweeter than honey. It's a good idea to explain to your supporters what you are doing.

Exercise B: Practice a Little Alinsky and a Lot of Carnegie

Within the next week, either using the experience undertaken to complete Exercise A or another one, promote a change in the way most comfortable to you. Then answer the following questions:

1. How would you describe your attempt along the Alinsky-Carnegie continuum?

2. Do you think you would have been more effective if you had behaved more like Alinsky or more like Carnegie?

3. Which of the two styles is more comfortable to you and why?

Rule #3:
RECOGNIZE AND OVERCOME THE FORCES OF "FOOLISH FREEDOM"

Making the world better requires individuals, whether stakeholders or players, to exercise their freedom in an enlightened and responsible way at every level, whether it is within a family, community, school, church, business, or government. In general, people will choose their private interest over the interest of society. Narrow self-interest, which we will call "foolish freedom," is the rule, while enlightened self-interest is the exception.

Actions to benefit the public interest occur in those few instances when people realize long-term interests require short-term sacrifices. Sometimes a crisis like a war or riot brings a community together, despite differing self-interests. Sometimes leaders overcome the obstacles of foolish freedom, providing solid guidance and making sacrifices to promote the good society. Civilization moves forward when this happens and backward when it fails to occur.

The United States was founded on the concept of freedom, and since that time, millions of people have traveled to this country to take advantage of a way of life that is not available everywhere in the world. Unfortunately, you can often times have too much of a good thing, and when that happens, people begin to take advantage of it. So even though we, as Americans, pride ourselves on the freedom we have, we must realize that too much of it can lead to the kinds of conditions we abhor, such as violent crime, deep-seated poverty, environmental degradation, and moral decay.

In order to improve and protect society, the "liberty" part of "life, liberty, and the pursuit of happiness" must be in harmony with the other two values. Freedom has to be viewed as only one part of the fabric of American society and culture, not as its totality. People have to work for themselves, but also for others. This kind of freedom carries responsibilities and a willingness to compromise for the public good.

This is not a revolutionary idea—it has been around forever and exists in every culture. In fact, no culture or society can survive unless people limit their self-interest enough to protect the public interest. That is an obvious, incontestable, and even mundane idea.

It is essential to realize that freedom can be an addiction that harms society and individuals. When it is pursued for itself with little regard for its personal or collective costs, it is "foolish freedom." Freedom becomes foolish when unaccompanied by purpose and responsibility.

Foolish freedom runs rampant in American society. Everywhere you turn, there are examples of foolish freedom. If you are not convinced of this, think about the list below and how it challenges the ideals of life, liberty, and the pursuit of happiness. It describes only a fraction of the acts of unenlightened self-interest taking place in our country today. In fact, almost all of our societal problems from crime, poor education, drug abuse, environmental degradation, illegal immigration, poor health, poverty, and unemployment are a result of selfishness and greed. Some might attribute it to the system of capitalism, and some might attribute it to lack of personal responsibility. Ultimately though, our problems are a result of the narrow pursuit of private interests against the need to protect the public interest.

The following short list demonstrates the negative effects of foolish freedom.

- Cigarette butts on the ground because smokers are too lazy to find an ashtray.

- Antibiotics that are over-prescribed, creating bacteria resistant to them.

- Disruptive students in our public schools because parents and teachers don't want to deal with problem kids.

- Young adults who stay in college or graduate school to remain on board their parents' gravy train.

- Business people who say "yes" to corporate welfare and "no" to social welfare for personal gain.

- Teenage pregnancies because making a baby before you're ready to assume adult responsibility is fun.

- Too little public transportation and car pooling because people want to go where they want, when they want.

- Talking on car phones, even though it causes traffic accidents because sitting in a car is a waste of time.

- Living in poverty and refusing to work for $7 an hour because the pay is too low.

- Surfing the TV and the Internet because many Americans have a short attention span and hyperactive fingers.

- College education for everyone, regardless of talent, motivation, and career goals, because college is believed to open more options.

- Drug, alcohol, gambling, Internet, and video game addiction because to be high is to be free.

- Hero worship of sports figures because people want to reach the same heights without the same work.

Don't worry if you are guilty of one or more of the actions listed above. We all exhibit some forms of foolish freedom—it is nearly impossible not to. No one in America is immune to foolish freedom. It is a part of American culture. Everywhere you turn—friends, the media, billboards, teachers, and the Internet (just to name a few)—acts of foolish freedom are being performed and suggested. Your job as a change agent is to promote the responsible exercise of freedom in the face of what seems to be the overwhelming drive to foolish freedom.

UBE STORIES:
Foolish Freedom at Any University

Players and stakeholders at colleges and universities around the country are willing victims of foolish freedom. Just think about these patterns of behavior:

- Professors place their pursuit of research publications above their under-graduate teaching duties.

- Professors skip their office hours because they "need" to take a break and play tennis.

- Students seek easy classes that meet afternoons on Tuesday and Thursday so they can have time to enjoy themselves at bars and in front of the TV.

- Professors choose to teach on Tuesday and Thursday so they don't have to come in on Monday, Wednesday, and Friday.

- University administrators bemoan the high consumption of alcohol on campus and then sell advertising space to beer companies in their sports facilities.

- Students drop a class because they may not get an A.

These examples of foolish freedom are at the heart of many of the problems faced by colleges and universities throughout the United States. Attempts to improve the quality of undergraduate education are continuously stymied by these and many other acts of selfishness by players and stakeholders alike.

Foolish freedom is not just a roadblock to improving society; it is also a force within yourself that you must confront before you can become an effective change agent. Once you realize this, you have learned the truth of the famous saying:

"We have met the enemy, and it is us." —Walter Kelly, *Pogo*

Change agents must fight their own tendencies toward foolish freedom. Many wanna-be change agents try to do too many things at once or take on a target they have no chance of reaching given their resources and time. Unwillingness to accept the constraints of reality is a form of foolish freedom and is a major danger to those who would change the world. Many wanna-be change agents underestimate how time-consuming, long, and unpleasant the road ahead will be.

As a change agent, you are confronted with foolish freedom both in front of and in back of you. Your first job is to gain control over yourself and a small group of supporters who share the same goal. This requires self-discipline and careful compromise. Once you have developed a clear and do-able objective shared by at least a few critical supporters, you are ready to move to change the policies of your organization and ultimately change the world. Just like athletes who have to fight their own internal demons and teams who have to forge themselves together as a unit, change agents organize themselves and their inner core of supporters before they can move ahead. To do this, they must exercise their freedom in a responsible way.

UBE STORIES:
Foolish Freedom by UBE Members

In our previous UBE Story, we listed the foolish freedom of undergraduates themselves as a source of the failure of college and universities to deliver on their mission as well as they should. As stakeholders, undergraduates could do much more to hold the feet of the faculty to the fire. However, they would be taking on more work and the risk of lower grades.

Foolish freedom has been an obstacle within UBE itself. Student organizations are notorious for disorganization, promising more than they can achieve, lack of leadership, and failure of members to accept responsibilities. All these manifestations of foolish freedom have characterized UBE over the years, even though the organization has survived and been successful. UBE is acknowledged as a key change agent in transforming Syracuse University from a place where faculty members spend too much time building their personal careers and the students too much time partying, to a place where students and faculty work more closely than ever before. But still the group is guilty of committing acts of foolish freedom:

- Publishing a course evaluation book with a limited number of courses because UBE members were too lazy to research more courses.

- Continuing to have only a small member base because the group does not work hard enough to recruit new students.

- Hosting a less than professional forum because UBE members did not spend enough time planning.

- Failing to attend meetings because members would rather see a basketball game.

- Working on too many projects at one time because each sounded like a good idea at the time.

Exercise C: Recognize and Confront Foolish Freedom

Choose an example where you are involved with some organization and answer the following questions.

1. What narrow self-interests prevent an organization (school, government, student group) from doing the right thing?

2. How are your own personal interests served and not served by the failure to take action?

3. Are you prepared to make the sacrifices necessary for something you would like your organization to do?

4. Will other members of your organizations make the sacrifices?

Rule #4:
GET YOUR PROBLEM ON THE AGENDAS OF PLAYERS

Getting a problem on the agenda of key players is always difficult. History is full of examples where those in control ignored the problem until it became so big that only costly action could resolve it. One classic example in the twentieth century is the emergence of Adolph Hitler in Germany during the 1930s. Those in power failed to place Hitler at the top of their agenda as a problem until it was too late to avoid World War II.

Your awareness of a problem is no guarantee the problem will even be recognized, let alone dealt with, by the players that can make a change. To get your problem on the agenda of an organization, whether it is a company, a nonprofit, or a government, means convincing at least one key player that the problem is important enough for the organization to take action. There are three basic reasons why those key players are likely to ignore you.

1. **Nobody wants to take responsibility for something wrong**. Players who are influential in an organization share responsibility for what that organization does. They have both the legal and moral responsibility to do what is best for the organization's stakeholders. The key players running a business organization are ultimately responsible for the safety of their workers. The board of directors of a nonprofit community center that allows drug dealers on the premises has not lived up to its responsibility to create a safe environment. To acknowledge a problem that is serious enough to warrant a change in the organization's behavior is to admit at least partial responsibility for failure.

2. **Nobody wants more work.** Players are busy people who have to satisfy other players. Recognizing a problem will mean longer meetings and other extra work. It will mean changing their current allocation of time and resources to confront the "new" problem.

3. **Nobody wants his or her power base threatened.** Never underestimate the insecurity of key players when potential problems are raised. The existence of the problem could threaten the power and self-interests of the key players. Pressure for change usually comes from less powerful players who are seeking to become more powerful. When Winston Churchill raised the question of the threat posed by Hitler, he was in political opposition. When Hitler proved Churchill right, Churchill became the most powerful player, the Prime Minister of Great Britain. Generally, influential players usually think it is better to deny the problem exists than to take a chance on what might happen if the problem is placed on the agenda of the organization.

The natural forces against change are considerable because most key players would prefer to keep new problems off their agendas. But change does occur. Despite their initial resistance, key players do recognize problems and work with others to solve them. This is true if the societal problem becomes increasingly serious over time. At some point, enough stakeholders are hurt by the problem that key players feel they need to act on it. For example, enough traffic fatalities on a stretch of road will lead to the consideration of lowering speed limits.

You will usually want to get the problem on the agenda of key players as early as possible. Waiting for the problem to become serious enough that key players see the need to act is not the way of a change agent. You want to be pre-emptive in order to end the suffering sooner, lower the cost of change, and increase the likelihood of success by taking early actions. But it is not just a matter of timing. It is possible that some problems will never be addressed until a key player is convinced to take the initiative.

You must act politically and strategically to convince key players that the problem must be addressed. The seven guidelines below can help you effectively convince key players that their organizations need to do something. The first five are a must; the last two are to be tried only if the first ones show no results and you want the problem on the agenda as soon as possible.

Guideline #1: Do your homework.

Conduct research with an open mind so you have your facts straight before you take action. You will need to complete the kind of research and analysis presented in the previous 11 chapters. But you still need to do more research by talking with others, consulting experts, and collecting information to make your pitch that the organization faces a serious problem.

Guideline #2: Develop simple and compelling arguments.

The second step is to provide evidence that stirs emotions. When faced with denial, you have to be ready to dispute that denial with clear, simple, and powerful arguments. Here is a list of ways to do that:

- Develop a brief statement that you make over and over again to drive home the seriousness of the problem.

- Provide specific horror stories showing the seriousness of the problem. Make sure to use real numbers expressed through percentages, which must be designed to have an emotional appeal that makes the player take notice.

- Paint a picture of how outraged stakeholders could embarrass the player in the media.

- First, test your arguments on those who agree that there is a problem. Then do the same thing on those who may not agree.

Guideline #3: Get the message out.

How and where your argument is presented must be chosen carefully. Keep your talking points brief, always stopping for feedback or questions. Make sure to prepare your written materials only after you have made your verbal presentations a few times; they will serve as the test marketing of your ideas. The written material should have very short paragraphs and lots of bullets and headings. But most importantly, make sure to use your knowledge, intuition, and skill when deciding how to get the message out. Remember the emphasis on brevity and clarity presented in Chapter 11.

Guideline #4: Find allies.

To find allies, you need to float your arguments about the seriousness of the problem. It is best to start testing your arguments with those you think would support your views. Ultimately, you have to develop a strategy to get as many allies as possible, both players and stakeholders.

Therefore, you should ask most of those who agree with you to tell others. The principle that an ally of your ally becomes your ally operates here. This self-reinforcing cycle of allies begetting allies can lead to the well-known bandwagon effect that will give your problem a ride to the top of key players' agendas.

However, you do not always want the help of all of your allies, because there is a converse principle: make sure your allies don't have a lot of enemies. You will probably have some allies who are enemies to important players. When this occurs, ask those supporters to remain quiet. This is in the nature of being a change agent. If they really support you, they will understand that you do not want to scare off powerful potential supporters.

Guideline #5: Prepare to benefit from external events.

In thinking about how you can build consensus, you must also consider the role of outside events. Frequently, outside events can heighten awareness and sensitivity to the problem more effectively than anything you do as an individual. Changing conditions, like a dip in enrollment for a university or runaway inflation, and highly visible events like a riot or a terrorist event, can be catalysts for community problem-solving.

Guideline #6: Propose a radical solution.

If you are having a tough time getting key players to put your problem on their agenda, you may want to try offering solutions to stimulate a debate that will increase the visibility of the problem. Floating such a proposal may have the effect of raising the problem even as the solution is being rejected.

Guideline #7: Use benchmarks for attention.

You may want to use benchmarking to help raise the visibility of a problem. By building support for a benchmark that identifies the problem, you can automatically push for it to become part of the agendas of the players.

Benchmarks can be useful because they present, in one statement, both measurements of the problem and goals indicating when the problem is remedied. If you can get some outside authority to state what a reasonable level of performance should be, you can play off of your players' fear, greed, and guilt to generate an increased awareness of the problem.

UBE STORIES:
Getting Student Grievances toward Faculty on the Administration's Agenda

In 1996, the members of UBE decided that a problem at Syracuse University was that students were afraid to approach professors about concerns over unfair treatment. For example, students who felt they received a grade lower than they deserved were afraid to talk to their professors about it. While at different times UBE uses each of the guidelines described in the last section of this chapter, this time they decided to **propose a radical solution** in order to get on players' agendas.

UBE proposed an all-university "ombudsman" (someone who is appointed to investigate citizens' complaints) position be established to highlight the problem. The chancellor thought that an ombudsman would generate more heat, not to mention expense, than light, but the idea got the attention of the administration. UBE immediately followed up to underscore the seriousness of the problem by presenting a list of 75 horror stories about how professors had refused to listen to students. The University's chancellor agreed there was a problem and put it on the University's agenda. The proposal of an ombudsman got the attention of the chancellor so he seriously examined the horror stories that were presented. Although he rejected the ombudsman idea, he did put the problem squarely on his agenda.

If leaders do nothing else, they set the agendas for their organizations. The chancellor brought the problem to the weekly meeting of college deans and asked them to develop a plan for their own colleges. In other words, after UBE placed it on his agenda, the chancellor then placed it on the agenda of the deans.

Exercise D: Get Your Problem on the Agenda of Players
Using the problem you have been working on in the last several exercises, develop a plan of action that will help promote the change you are looking for. You can do this by completing the tasks listed below.

1. List the players who will determine whether a change occurs.

2. Discuss three strategies to get on one of the player's agenda.

Rule #5: BUILD A WINNING COALITION

You may find that just getting players to be aware of a problem is enough to set the wheels of change in motion as in the UBE example described on the last page. However, sometimes change agents have to do much more. They must get those players with the most power and the highest interest in their proposed change to be on their side. This is what politics is all about—building a winning coalition.

To build a winning coalition, you will need to complete the Prince chart described in Chapter 9 of this book and the strategies suggested in Chapter 10.

Your ultimate goal is to get many powerful players to support the action you want to see your organization undertake. How you do that depends on a variety of strategies that include making persuasive arguments, offering compromises, and promising to help players out on topics that are of interest to them. The change agent is always in a weak position since most players favor the status quo that gave them their power in the first place. Therefore, you should be always willing to accept a compromise. Half a loaf or even a tenth of a loaf is better than nothing.

UBE STORIES:
Building a Winning Coalition

UBE created a Prince chart to develop a strategy to get a winning coalition on its side to deal with the problem of student grievances through an ombudsman. The chart revealed that the chances were slim to none. Led by the chancellor's firm opposition and high power, other players generally agreed with his position. Only UBE supported the proposal.

Using this chart, it was clear that once the chancellor made his position known, there would be no ombudsman. UBE could have kept pressuring for such an office, but its goal was to help students communicate better with faculty over matters of concern. It continued to push the ombudsman idea for a while and then developed a plan to act more or less as an ombudsman on its own. As a result, the chancellor and deans agreed that they would prefer to have control over the process, and they developed a plan for a formal grievance procedure in each school. By changing its policy proposal, UBE was able to build a winning coalition for strong university action.

Exercise E:

Using the same policy problem you used in Exercise D, complete the following.

1. Complete a Prince chart.

2. Discuss how you would go about building a winning coalition among the players on the chart so that enough are moved toward a strong supporting position.

Profile of a Change Agent

Diana Aubourg Millner

Diana Aubourg Millner is the Executive Director of Save Africa's Children and is an example of a powerful change agent. She writes the following about how PAF 101 and this book gave her the tools to be effective:

"When I took PAF 101 as a freshman at SU, I knew nothing about the HIV/AIDS epidemic in Africa. I was a wide-eyed, domestically focused 'do-gooder.' I managed to temper my idealism with a public policy 'toolkit' assembled in PAF 101 through modules demanding critical thinking and keen, if not neurotic, attention to detail. I expanded this toolkit as a Policy Studies major—navigating through core courses and my selection as a Harry S. Truman Scholar, Remembrance Scholar, and Public Policy and International Affairs (PPIA) Fellow.

After my first semester at MIT's Department of Urban Studies and Planning, I shifted focus from urban policy to international development planning. In the two years leading to graduate school, I became immersed in advocacy around a 'do-gooder' issue that flickered dimly on the world radar screen: millions of Africans dying of AIDS and millions of children orphaned. I now run one of the largest African American faith-based organizations supporting orphans and vulnerable children in Africa. Since 2001, we have directly assisted over 350 programs in Africa serving AIDS orphans. I work with people on the ground in Africa and interface with policymakers, practitioners, and development experts. I am frequently the youngest of my colleagues.

I find myself swimming in an enormous problem that would appear to defy all the basic principles of policy analysis. But I have dipped into my 'toolkit' at every turn, from my graduate research fieldwork in Africa to representing my organization at international policy and advocacy forums. Passion (or compassion) is simply not enough to 'solve' a world problem of epic proportions such HIV/AIDS. But conviction matched with concrete skills may lead to a seat at the decision making table or an opportunity, however daunting, to become a true change agent."

Chapter 13

Editorials and Public Policy Analysis

YOUR GOAL   To identify, assess, and write the five types of public policy analysis found in editorials.

Introduction

A good analyst uses the following five types of analysis when discussing a public policy issue.

1.   Monitoring societal conditions

2.   Explaining societal conditions

3.   Forecasting societal conditions

4.   Evaluating societal conditions

5.   Prescribing public policy

This chapter will help you to identify which types of public policy analysis are presented in editorials and op-ed articles.

Monitoring Societal Conditions

Monitoring societal conditions is the process of observing and recording what is happening in society that gives rise to public policy issues. Like the biologist who carefully observes nature, the public policy analyst collects information about society.

Guidelines for Monitoring

1. **Present clear and precise information.** Look for a clear and specific description of societal conditions.

2. **Give information that is as complete as possible.** Testing for completeness can be done by answering three questions:

   a. Does the information provided allow for a comparison of conditions over time? It is better to know the number of traffic fatalities for each of the past five years than for only the most recent year.

   b. Does the information make an effort to cover all parts of the society, or does it deal with only certain areas or groups? In a study of New York State, reports on traffic fatalities only in New York City would not be adequate.

   c. Does the information provide a basis for comparison between areas?

3. **Provide evidence that the information is accurate.** Cite books, articles, documents, or surveys used. Numbers and information provided without documentation cannot be trusted as much as those with documentation. Accuracy is always a problem in measuring social conditions, and the more known about how that information was collected the better.

Explaining Societal Conditions

Explaining societal conditions is describing what factors contribute to the conditions monitored in society. If you have ever missed a curfew set by your parents, you may have attempted to explain why you were late. Explanation as a form of public policy analysis is similar, since it requires you to give the reasons why society is the way it is. The examples on the next page provide several explanations of different societal conditions.

> **Examples of Explaining Societal Conditions**
>
> The Congress and administration are not willing to suffer the political consequences of cutting, spending, or raising taxes.
>
> As disabled advocacy groups gain publicity, more people want to find out how to make use of their services.
>
> Cuts in funding for food stamps, welfare benefits, and housing subsidies have made housing unaffordable for the poor.

Explaining why a condition exists is quite difficult, because most societal conditions are caused by a large number of factors. For instance, the number of traffic fatalities in a particular area can be affected by the weather, the driving speed, and even the health of the economy. Research can give a general indication of which factors are important, but even the most elaborate studies fail to give absolutely complete explanations.

Guidelines for Good Explaining

1. **Cite as many relevant factors as possible.** Most societal conditions are caused by a large number of interacting factors. For example, juvenile delinquency may be caused by broken homes, peer pressure, low self-esteem, and several other factors. Therefore, single-factor explanations are almost always inaccurate. An attempt to consider a large number of factors is a sign that the analyst is trying to be as careful as possible in developing explanations. The following categories of factors should be considered: (1) economic, (2) geographic, (3) sociological, (4) political, and (5) psychological.

2. **Cite academic or government sources to support the factors you list.** For almost every public policy issue, studies exist that identify the causes of the conditions that have generated the issue. These studies are undertaken by scholars working in universities, research organizations, and also by government agencies. For example, in 1986, The Final Report of the Attorney General's Commission on Pornography contended that pornography is one of the factors responsible for a growing number of rapes and acts of violence against women.

Chapter 2 will tell you how to locate these studies in the library. A good explanation will cite studies that demonstrate which factors contribute most to a societal condition.

Forecasting Societal Conditions

Forecasting societal conditions is predicting what societal conditions will be like in the future. Like the weather forecaster who attempts to tell you in the middle of the week what the weekend weather will be, the public policy analyst makes forecasts about what society will look like several months, one year, or even ten years, down the road. Unfortunately, like the weather forecaster, uncertainty surrounds forecasts of social conditions. The further into the future the prediction, the greater the uncertainty. The examples below provide several forecasts of different societal conditions.

Examples of Forecasting Societal Conditions

The American federal debt will double within the next five years.

The number of calls to the Office of Advocate for the Disabled will increase by an average of 5 percent per month over the next year as more people find out about the referral service.

The number of homeless people will increase by 10 percent annually over the next three years.

Discussions of public policy issues are concerned with the future. All public policies are undertaken either to change future social conditions or to prevent changes. Forecasting, therefore, is critical to any public policy analyst.

Guidelines for Good Forecasting

1. **Be clear with respect to what is being forecast and the time frame of the forecast.** Forecasts are incomplete if they are unclear about the amount of increase, the time frame, and where the change will occur.

2. **Cite academic or government authorities if possible.** The best forecasts are backed up by government or academic studies and are made by individuals and groups who have expertise and have no vested interest in the conclusion of the forecast. A particularly useful approach is to find several forecasts by experts and to consider all their conclusions.

3. **Make reasoning behind the forecast clear.** If you are unable to find academic or government authorities to support your forecast, you will need to make clear your own reasoning for the forecast. Basically, you will make one of two types of forecasts:

a. Things will continue as they have been in the past. For example, "For each of the next five years, traffic fatalities in New York State will rise 5 percent per year" could be based on a trend over the past decade that shows a 5 percent a year increase.

b. Things will be different from what they have been in the past. For example, "The number of traffic deaths in New York State will decline by 5 percent a year over the next five years because of increased use of seatbelts."

Both forecasts could be based on the same historical information over the past ten years. However, forecast B assumes that increased use of seatbelts will cause a change in the historical trend. Forecast A, on the other hand, assumes that increased seatbelt use will not make a major difference.

Evaluating Societal Conditions

Evaluating societal conditions is judging whether conditions in society are desirable or undesirable. A public policy analyst might conclude that the number of traffic fatalities is too high, or, if the trend is downward, that conditions are improving. Like teachers who grade *your* performance, public policy analysts determine whether society is performing up to levels they consider adequate.

Evaluation of societal conditions is important because the conclusion reached about whether there is too much crime, drug abuse, unemployment, or any other undesirable social condition leads to decisions about whether new public policies are needed. The examples below provide several evaluations of different societal conditions.

Examples of Evaluating Societal Conditions

The federal debt will unfairly burden future generations with staggering bills.

People who call the referral service benefit from being directed to the resource office that can best help them.

Too many homeless people die from exposure and lack of proper medical care.

Guidelines for Good Evaluating

1. **Be clear in identifying goals that should be used to judge social conditions.** Good public policy analysis requires a clear statement of what societal conditions are desired. For example, those supporting the mandatory seat belt law in New York State have the goal of fewer traffic fatalities. In many cases, the analyst takes for granted that the reader understands the importance of the goal of the analysis.

2. **Consider all major goals that are relevant to the public policy issue.** Most policy issues involve many goals, some consistent with one another, some in conflict. For example, a discussion of the mandatory seatbelt law can begin with the goal of preserving human life, but it should identify other goals which may or may not be in conflict with saving lives. Some of these are (1) individual freedom, which many feel is reduced by the law; (2) the respect of government itself because of the difficulty in enforcing the law; (3) increased costs to the taxpayers resulting from the enforcement costs; and (4) reduced car insurance premiums.

Prescribing Public Policy

Prescribing public policy is advocating what government action should be taken to promote good societal conditions. For example, the analyst might prescribe a mandatory seatbelt law, as the New York State government did in 1984, to reduce traffic fatalities. Like a medical doctor who prescribes an antibiotic to cure an infection, the public policy analyst prescribes a government action to reduce undesirable societal conditions or to promote desirable ones. The examples below provide several prescriptions for different societal conditions.

Examples of Prescribing Public Policies

The federal government should double the gasoline tax.

The Office of Advocate for the Disabled should launch a publicity campaign to inform the public of the services they provide.

The amount of federal funds allocated to low-income housing programs should be increased by 50 percent.

Guidelines for Good Prescribing

1. **Provide a clear prescription**. The analyst must be very clear about which policy is being recommended and at what level of government. Also, a goal must not be confused with a prescription.

2. **Provide several alternatives to the favored prescription.** While the analysis may clearly endorse a specific policy, it should also examine the alternatives. This will demonstrate that the analysis includes all the relevant factors. For example, if an analysis favors mandatory seatbelt legislation, it should discuss such alternatives as requiring air bags or spending more money on safety education.

3. **Assess the desirable and undesirable consequences of the prescription and the alternatives.** For each prescription suggested, the analyst should consider the good and bad consequences that might result directly or indirectly from the policy. Some attempt should be made to weigh the pluses and minuses for each policy and to reach a conclusion about why the favored prescription is preferred. For example, a mandatory seatbelt law may reduce traffic, but it may have the undesirable consequence of limiting individual freedom. An air bag law might reduce fatalities even more, but it would be much more costly.

Chapter 14

Format for a Quantitative Research Paper

YOUR GOAL   To conduct and write a study using quantitative data.

Introduction

Decision-makers in government, business, and the non-profit world frequently need to acquire information in quantitative form. The reasons for this are discussed in Chapter 16. Sometimes the data is generated by surveys, which are discussed in Chapter 4 and Chapter 15, while sometimes the data comes from records or direct observations.

This chapter assumes that you are conducting research and writing a report for a public policy client under the supervision of an instructor. Its purpose is to guide you to complete your data collection and analysis efficiently. It also provides a specific format that will make your report as useful to the client as possible. If your client prefers a different format, you should adjust accordingly. However, the format presented in this chapter should be followed if the client does not indicate a preference or if your instructor requires it.

The chapter begins with some suggestions on a variety of topics. It then moves on to the important question of planning and scheduling. The last section provides specific format guidelines that are very detailed.

General Guidelines

Experience is clearly the best teacher, but since you are probably undertaking this type of project for the first time, you have little experience upon which to build. Fortunately, we can learn from the mistakes of others. Students who have written reports and have learned the hard way provide the hints listed below. Take their lessons seriously.

Organizing Your Project

Selecting a Project

In selecting a project, use the following criteria:

- Your ability to complete all tasks required in the project
- Your interest in the subject with which the project is concerned
- Your ability to learn about the subject in order to complete the project
- Your ability to communicate with the prospective client
- Your ability to understand the objectives of the client
- Your ability to anticipate the technical pitfalls of the project
- Your ability to get to and from the client and other sites necessary to do your research
- Your access to a telephone for any necessary calls

Clients

- Get to know your agency
- Keep control of your client
- Be specific in your contract; don't let the client add tasks beyond what is initially agreed
- Learn the technical language of the client
- Do not pay for client's work such as phone calls or postage
- Do not be surprised if secretaries and others give you a hard time
- Maintain close contact with the client
- Do not take the client's behavior personally

- Call to confirm appointments within 24 hours of the agreed time

- Do not be misled by titles

- Make the client keep deadlines

- If the client is giving data or membership lists, acquire them immediately and check for quality. Don't believe in promises of lists or other information until you actually have your hands on them

Project

- Prioritize goals at the outset

- Do not underestimate the amount of time required

- Set firm, specific deadlines, and keep them

- Be specific with your client about the final product

- Do not rely on the client for most of the information

- Make sure that any information provided by the client is accurate and current

- Double check your data with the client before analysis

- Keep your paperwork organized

- Beware of sensitive information and keep it confidential

- Ask permission to quote

- Complete the final draft 48 hours before it is due

- Use your agenda as a planning and time management device

Surveying

- Subject knowledge is essential to good questions

- Pre-test your survey

- Make sure the target population is appropriate

- Anticipate delays in getting surveys back

- Get permission from the respondent to conduct the survey

- Make sure respondents' privacy and rights are respected

In General

- Complete a bibliography and talk to experts so you can learn as much as possible about the subject

- Be prepared for such serious computer problems as lost data files and unreadable disks

- Check with instructor early; keep notes

- Know your way around the area you're working in

- Do not be a spoiled brat

- Watch out for serious roadblocks; alert instructor at once

Planning and Scheduling Research Projects

This section is key to your success because poor plans and poor scheduling will lead to missed deadlines and a poor report. Follow the guidelines below.

In General

- You will have to provide your own transportation to and from the agency.

- Inquire about agency funds for any additional supplies required to complete the project.

- Keep all appointments with your agency contact.

- Your dress and conduct must, at all times, convey your position as a professional researcher carrying out an important project. Your behavior reflects upon you and your program.

- Type your final report error-free and of presentation-quality which means setting sufficient time for proofing.

- Make three copies of your agency report. One copy is for your program's records, one will be sent to the agency, and one is for your files. It may be helpful to you in seeking an internship, a job, a scholarship, or admission to graduate school.

- Review past projects on file in the office to see what a good project looks like and what has been done previously for your agency and related agencies.

- Maintain close contact with your instructor. Completing the project for this course is like completing a job. Your instructor is your boss. When you make an appointment, keep it or call the office at least 24 hours ahead of time to cancel and reschedule.

- Keep class time free of any other commitments, even when no formal class is held. Do not schedule client appointments at that time. Plan to contact the course professor during designated class times.

Agenda

The agenda is a critical self-management tool to make sure you have carefully planned the activities you need to undertake to complete a high quality project. Discuss the agenda with your client as a way of communicating what you are planning to do and to see if the client has any comment on your plans.

The agenda will also be reviewed by the course professor to ensure that you are on track. Carefully check the syllabus for the due dates of the agenda.

A sample agenda appears on the next page. Note that this agenda is from a completed project. You will need to save your first agenda and prepare a final one for your debriefing report. Use a Microsoft Excel spreadsheet and use a format similar to the one on the next page.

Sally Student

PAF 315, Spring 2006

Project: Effectiveness of ABC Organization

Client: Jane Doe, ABC Organization of Central New York

Item	Deadline	Date Done	Time Planned	Actual Time	Comments
First meeting with client	9/4	9/22	1	1	Overall plan for research determined
Diagnostic test, review spreadsheet commands	9/1	9/27	5	9	Had forgotten more than I realized
Second meeting with client	9/12	9/12	1	1	Questionnaire discussed and more planning
Telephone calls with Jane	9/15	9/14	2	2	Confirmation of who will do what
Contract signed	9/6	9/6	1	2	Client out of town for 2 days
Preparation of spreadsheet programs	9/30	9/30	2	6	Programs had to be revised
Follow-up meeting with client	10/1	10/1	1	1	
Third meeting with client	10/7	10/7	2	2	Revise plans; collect questionnaires
Agency paper	10/10	10/10	4	6	Delay for printer to be repaired
Annotated bibliography	10/10	10/10	2	2	Library research completed
Call school for confirmation	10/10	10/13	1	1	Had to make several calls before making contact
Faculty report	10/11	10/14	4	6	Faculty not in office during scheduled hours
Collection of school surveys	10/11	10/11	1	1	118 questionnaires
Received pre-surveys from other schools	10/16	10/16	1	1	92 questionnaires
Received other post-surveys	10/23	10/23	1	1	83 questionnaires
Data input 25 cases	11/8	11/8	5	7	Pre-test at first school; entry didn't work right at first
Data input 25 cases	11/11	11/11	5	6	Pre-test at second school; had to wait for a computer
Update agenda	11/12	11/12	1	1	
Data input 50 cases	11/13	11/13	5	6	Post-test at first school
Data input the remainder of cases	11/13	11/13	5	4	Post-test at second school; finally getting the hang of it!
Meeting with client	11/14	11/15	1	2	Client out of town on scheduled meeting day
Graph creations	11/15	11/15	5	3	Lots of false starts with charting program
Graph creations	11/16	11/18	10	12	Chart program not working as well as first time
First draft of Research Paper	11/22	11/23	3	4	Extra research needed
Revise draft	11/23	11/24	2	3	Reorganization needed
Make extra copies of Research Paper	11/23	11/23	1	1	
Draft Final Paper	11/24	11/24	1	2	More to it than I thought at first
Memo to Client	11/24	11/24	1	2	Kept thinking of extra things to say
Letter to faculty advisor	12/1	12/1	1	1	
TOTALS			75	96	

Format for the Report

Report Standards

- Font Size—The paper should be typed in size 12 Times New Roman Font.

- Do not right-justify; instead, use a ragged-right margin.

- A cover sheet will be provided by the course instructor. Use this cover sheet or a clean copy of it for your title page.

- Number each page, beginning with the Introduction. Use a footer that summarizes the title, and include the date. The footer should read: Title of Paper, Month Year, Page Number (Senior Citizen Housing Needs Assessment, November 1999, Page 7).

- Footers—Begin footers on the Introduction page. To do this, insert a section break. (At the end of the Executive Summary, go to insert, break, and select next page under section break types) then make your footer on the Introduction page. To do the footer, at the end of it type the word "Page", and then click insert page number on the footer toolbar.

- Footers in the Appendix—Should be the same as the rest of the paper, but the page numbers in the Appendix should be the roman numeral of the Appendix, and then the page number within that Appendix. If Appendix II is data frequencies, and you are on the third page of data frequencies, the footer should end with "Appendix II-3"

- Bind the report by placing one large staple in the upper left-hand corner of the report.

- Make the report a self-contained document; do not refer to some print-out in the body of any paper.

- Place statistics associated with any figure immediately within, below, or beside the discussion, not on a separate page.

- Do not print in any color other than black and white, since other colors will not copy clearly. You may use shadings and hatch-marks in your graphs. Commentary must appear on the same page as the corresponding figure. Pay attention to how it will photocopy.

- Use simple, clear graphics.

- On the Executive Summary, at the end of each finding you have the sample size (n=?). In the findings section, the rest of the finding statement is identical, but do not put the sample size in the finding because it is under the title of the graph.

- Findings on Executive Summary—Double space between findings, which should be single spaced if more than one line. If single spacing between the findings will make the Executive Summary fit on one page, do that.

- Under quality of data in the Methods section, discuss representativeness and accuracy in at least two different paragraphs. Remember: representativeness is how well your sample represents the target population. Accuracy is the degree to which the information is "truthful." There can be many reasons for raising suspicions about truthfulness of data, including unclear questions, lying, and sloppy record-keeping.

- Difference between n and N—In your report, you need to tell readers the sample size for each of your findings. You will use a lowercase n when the respondents are a sample or part of the target population. An uppercase N is used when the number of respondents equals the entire target population.

- Graphing guidelines—Always make bar graphs. If there are more than 6 bars, use the horizontal bar graph. No pie charts. No color, no gridlines, no legends. Put data values at the top of each column. Pay attention to labeling. See Chapter 16.

- To Rank or Not to Rank in Bar Graphs—If the category on the x-axis of a graph is nominal, such as race or gender, the bars should be descending in height. If the variable is ordinal, such as age or how much the respondent agrees with something, the bars should stay in order of the variable (very dissatisfied at one end, very satisfied at the other end). One exception is yes/no, which should appear in that order.

- Percentages in findings—Don't use decimals in percentages. If it would round to zero, say <1%.

- Single space within paragraphs and double space between each paragraph. Don't indent. Do not write in the first person anywhere in your report.

- Utilize—Don't use that word for the rest of your life.

- Prepare a perfectly clean and properly formatted paper. No errors of spelling, style, or formatting are acceptable. Hand-made corrections are not acceptable.

- Each of the main sections of the report must be in all capitals and centered on the page. They are: EXECUTIVE SUMMARY, INTRODUCTION, METHODS, FINDINGS, and APPENDICES.

Title Page

Begin the title 4 inches from the top of the page, centered between left and right sides. Type the title with a font similar to "Times New Roman" in all capitals, bold-face, using a type size of 14-20, depending on the length of the title. Keep the title short and informative.

Avoid unnecessary words such as "study," "survey," and "report." In other words, do not produce titles such as "Report on a Survey Study of the Client Satisfaction with XYZ Agency." Instead, write "Client Satisfaction with XYZ Agency."

Starting 3 inches from the bottom of the page, type a centered sub-title in bold-face using initial capitals and the same font, and about half the size of the main title, according to the following format:

A Study Conducted for the [Agency Client]
[Further identification of particular office, if appropriate]
by [Your Name]
Month Year

See the sample title page on next page.

SENIOR CITIZEN HOUSING NEEDS
ASSESSMENT

A Study Conducted for the Tully Housing Authority
by Jennifer Ayers
November 1999

EXECUTIVE SUMMARY

Write this section after the rest of the report is finished. Use your word processor to copy and paste from the rest of the report. Begin the Executive Summary on a new page. The title and the subtitle at the top of the Executive Summary page should follow the sample on page 171 using bold-faced type. It consists of a title, the name of the agency, your name, and the date.

The Executive Summary consists of three paragraphs:

1. One paragraph summarizing the Introduction to the report.

2. One paragraph summarizing the Methods for gathering and analyzing data.

3. One paragraph summarizing substantive Findings.

Boldface and underline the words **Introduction**, **Methods**, and **Findings**. Use the same phrasing in the Executive Summary that appears in the body of the report.

Here are some general principles for your Executive Summary.

- Do not use the words 'I' or 'we.'

- The Executive Summary should be one page but should fill up the entire page. You may use 10 instead of 12-point font size. (Use 12 for the rest of the paper.)

- Use past tense, since you are reporting a study that has already been undertaken.

First Paragraph: Summarizing Introduction

- Good standard first sentences are: "This study reports information gathered through a survey conducted for _____. The study will assist (the name of the agency) to _____.

- The first paragraph must always mention how the client will use the information.

Second Paragraph: Summarizing Methods

- Do not use "approximately," especially when referring to a sample or findings.

- In the Methods section, do not mention the questions or topics of the survey. These items will be discussed in the Findings section.

- Be specific about the target population and the sample. Give numbers of each. Be specific about how a sample was chosen and what percentage of the sample responded.

- The Methods section should not contain findings except for the demographics of the respondents. In most cases, do not put the demographics, such as male-female distribution, in the Findings section unless the client requests it.

- Do not write in the Methods section that you tabulated the data or used a spreadsheet. This information is redundant and irrelevant (as is this sentence).

Third Paragraph: Summarizing Findings

- If possible, the findings should be listed in descending order of importance.

- The findings listed in the Executive Summary must be identical to the actual finding headlines in the Findings section of the report.

Senior Citizen Housing Needs Assessment
Tully Housing Authority
by Jennifer Ayers
November 1999

EXECUTIVE SUMMARY

Introduction: This study reports information gathered through a survey conducted for the Tully Housing Authority. The results will be included in a report to the United Way and the agency's Board of Directors. The report will be used to help assess the program and develop new policies.

Methods: The data for the study was generated through a telephone survey of individuals who have used the program over the past two years. Respondents were selected by choosing every third name from a master list of clients. From the target population of 304, a simple random sample of 100 was selected, and 74 responses were obtained. In the sample, 65% of the respondents were female, compared to 71% female in the target population.

Findings: Of the 74 respondents:

1. 82% received care from the Home Care Division for more than 6 months.

2. 57% learned about the agency from their doctor or hospital staff.

3. 80% of the patients indicated they received Very Good or Good services from the agency's home care nurses.

4. 86% of those receiving physical therapy found the services to be either Very Good or Good.

5. 78% of the patients have never had to reach agency staff members after hours or on weekends.

6. 92% of the patients have never had a problem reaching staff members.

INTRODUCTION

Provide background information about your project. Typical points which may be addressed include:

- Why the research was undertaken
- A definition of the problems being studied
- Any research discussion with client
- Previous research for which this is a follow-up
- A future larger project for which this is a pilot study
- What uses the agency will make of this report

(Not **all** of these points need to be covered.)

The first sentence of your Executive Summary should be used as the first sentence of your Introduction. Do not provide background information on your client or agency; they already know about themselves.

METHODS

The purpose of the Methods section is to explain to the reader, in as much organized detail as possible, the following:

- How you obtained the data
- How accurately the data represents what it is supposed to represent

These two topics apply regardless of the type of data you are using—whether published information, information supplied by agency records, or surveys you are conducting yourself. Divide your Methods section using the two sub-headings below.

How Data Was Collected

In describing how you obtained the data, be as precise as possible. The test is this: Could the reader collect the data after reading your description? To ensure this, here are some guidelines:

- For *published sources,* provide full documentation and describe how the author of the source collected the data.
- *For information provided by the client,* describe the procedures used to obtain the data. Interview the client and others involved in collecting the

information. Be sure to include all collection forms and to discuss how the data was recorded, and if relevant, include the final form you received.

- *For surveys*, you need to follow the guidelines in Chapters 4 and 15. Organize your discussion into the following categories:

    1. Instrument Design. Describe how the survey instrument (question-naire) was designed and tested. Discuss who wrote it. Indicate if there was any pilot testing.

    2. Target Population and Sample. Define the target population and describe the sample selection process.

    3. Method of Contact. Procedures used to contact the respondents.

Quality of the Data

Discuss the quality of the data in terms of both its representativeness and its accuracy. Representativeness refers to whether the data provide a complete picture. If the data comprises all of the available information, then by definition it is representative. However, if it is a sample of the complete data, then you must discuss whether or not the sample reflects the total set of information. Accuracy refers to whether the data provided a "true picture of reality." Mistakes in recording information or deliberate misinformation or a lack of clarity about the data being collected detract from accuracy.

- When using data from published sources: You can comment on the reputation of the publisher or the author. A discussion of how vested interest might play a role is frequently required. The degree to which the source is cited by others and the history of the publication—how many previous editions—is also useful.

- When using data from agency records: Maintain a healthy skepticism since the agency is likely to argue that the data is accurate. Ask questions, such as "How many cases should you have?" and "How many do you have?" Frequently, an agency will claim that it has all of the records of its clients but when you look at the actual list, it is far fewer than the agency reports it has. Ask to look at the original documents. Look out for incomplete and illegible records. Ask how long the data has been collected and who is responsible for the data collection. Ask whether or not the information is sent to government agencies or funders.

- When using survey data which you collect or is collected by the agency or someone else: Assess the degree to which the sample is likely to reflect the target population by comparing distributions on key variables.

Comment on whether or not the wording of the questions or the method of the contact may have introduced systematic bias or caused the respondent not to provide an honest response.

Remember that there will always be questions about accuracy. Discuss them fully. If possible, provide suggestions on how to improve the accuracy of the data by improving data collection procedures. If appropriate, include revised forms and survey instruments in an appendix. The next pages contain an example of how the Methods section should be organized for a survey.

METHODS

How Data was Collected

Instrument Design: The survey was created by the National Foundation for Consumer Credit. Because the Consumer Credit Counseling Service of Central New York had conducted similar survey studies, the national organization used its previous surveys as a guide in creating the new national standard survey. Therefore, the survey used could not be altered in any way, because the national agency wanted to compare results between agencies throughout the United States. The researcher was not notified of any pilot testing of the final survey.

Target Population and Sample: The target population consists of 5,058 Consumer Credit Counseling clients from the committees of Syracuse, Fort Drum, Utica, Binghamton, Colonie, Vestal, and Albany in New York State. The agency provided a sampling frame that included 1,277 clients. These clients were selected by printing the mailing labels of each counselor's clients at each location. Then, in an effort to represent each counselor equally, the first column of each counselor's label list was taken as the sampling frame. This represented a 25% random sample of the clientele at each location. A total of 394 responses were received out of 1,277 mailings (a 31% response rate).

Method of Contact: The questionnaires were mailed to the sample and mailed back to the agency. The agency then opened the responses to be sure that clients did not include their monthly payments in the envelopes. The agency also photocopied any questionnaires on which the clients reported problems that should be given immediate attention.

Quality of the Data

The sample population appears to be representative of the target population. The percentages received from each area closely match the percentages sent out to each area. There may be some error in this data because 131 out of the 394 respondents did not indicate on their questionnaire which area they were from. This figure represents 33% of the total number of questionnaires received. The design of the survey may have affected this statistic. The question on office location was not clearly stated or visible. When conducting next year's survey, the client should recommend to the national organization that the questionnaire be altered to make that item more easily seen.

Figure 14.1: Comparing Target Population to Sample (main sources or responses)

Location	Target Population Location N=5058	Sample Indicating Their Location N=263	Difference
Syracuse	39%	39%	0
Utica	13%	11%	+2
Binghamton	18%	18%	0
Albany	30%	32%	-2

Those clients who included their name and detailed complaints about service were contacted by the agency to try to alleviate their problems as quickly as possible. This did not sacrifice the study's confidentiality statement because there was no space on the survey to place the respondent's name. When respondents did include their name, the agency took this as a request for immediate assistance. Because only 4% of the respondents provided their names and used the survey as a way to request action on their specific problems, this is not evidence of an overrepresentation of negative responses.

There were a total of 394 respondents in the survey. A small number of respondents left some of the questions blank. This explains why the frequencies are not the same for each graph. The sample size represents the number of people who actually answered a given question.

FINDINGS

In this section, provide the agency with a brief summary of the conclusions of the study. Present findings as a series of short briefings that take the following form, in order, on a separate page for each finding:

- **Headline:** A brief statement summarizing a key point. The key point is usually the largest category (or group of categories) in a given finding. For example, if you find that 10 percent of respondents are "very satisfied" and 55 percent are "satisfied" with an agency, a headline could read: "65 percent of respondents are satisfied or very satisfied with the agency."

- **Figure:** A bar graph using the format in the sample graph on page 179 properly labeled and numbered consecutively within the report. **Follow the formatting guidelines below:**

  - Entitle the graph and label both axes

  - Include "N =" under the title

  - Use percentages, not raw numbers

  - Include data labels

  - Clear the background of the graph

  - Do not code the category labels on the X-axis. For example, write "Male" or "Female," not "M" and "F."

  - Identify the source for each graph

- **Comment:** Add a comment only if necessary. In most cases, there will be no comments. Do not repeat the headline or summarize the findings presented in the figure. The purpose of a comment is to assist the reader in understanding the data presented in the figure by providing information that the reader may not have. Here are some of the primary types of comments you might make:

  - The data used is flawed by a poor sample or a poor question or missing responses.

  - A statistical analysis reveals that the pattern in the data presented is related to some other variable such as sex, age, location, or participation. This is a discussion of confounding variables. In some cases, you may want to put cross-tabulation tables in the comment or in the appendix to support your discussion.

  - The finding under discussion is related to a previous or subsequent finding.

If possible, list the findings in order of importance to the agency, starting with the most important. If that is not possible or appropriate, present the findings in some other logical order, such as the order in which the information was gathered (as from a questionnaire), or in order from the most surprising to least surprising.

For surveys and data sets with large numbers of variables, you may want to group variables or responses into findings. If you wish to present a large number of results that do not warrant any comment, place them in an Appendix with a brief discussion in the Findings section.

Do not provide prescriptions, recommendations, or evaluations in the comments or anywhere else in the report.

See the sample finding presented in proper format on the next page.

(Sample finding presented with a bar graph for a figure)

FINDINGS

1. 74% of the agency's clients have used the agency's services for less than 100 hours.

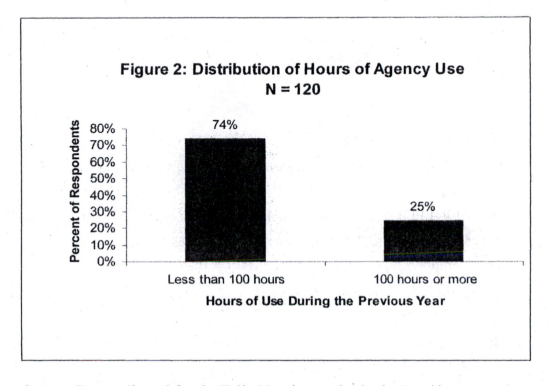

Figure 2: Distribution of Hours of Agency Use
N = 120

Source: Data collected for the Tully Housing Authority by Jennifer Ayers, Research Project, Syracuse University, November 1999.

Comment: Many clients may not be aware of all the services available, since many respondents were unaware that the Valley Service Office was actually a part of the agency's services. Consequently, these findings may under-represent the actual number of hours of agency use by clients.

APPENDICES

Clearly label and consecutively number the Appendices, using Roman numerals for each Appendix and Arabic page numbers for each section. For example, number page 1 of Appendix I as I-1; number page 6 of Appendix III as III-6. Appendices may contain copies of raw and untyped draft, samples, or similar material if they are appropriate and legible.

Include the following items in the Appendices if available (all the items listed below are rarely included in one report):

- Blank questionnaire.

- Data frequencies listed on a copy of the questionnaire.

- Individual responses to open-ended questions with similar answers grouped.

- CODEBOOK if a computer-readable data set is used. (See next page for a sample codebook.)

- Computer printed listings of data if fewer than 5 pages.

- Technical information on the results of statistical analysis and documentary research.

- Sample of final product prepared as part of the project. For example, a cleaned listing or a revised questionnaire.

CODEBOOK

COLUMN	FIELD NAME	DEFINITION	FORMAT
A	ID	Student's identification number	Value
B	LAST NAME	Student's last name	Text
C	FIRST NAME	Student's first name	Text
D	BIRTHDAY	Date of birth NA = Not available	Date
E	SEX	Sex of student	Text
F	TUTOR	Willing to volunteer for tutoring project? Y = Yes; N = No; NA = Not available	Text
G	CLEAN	Willing to volunteer for house cleaning project? Y = Yes; N = No; NA = Not available	Text

Chapter 15

Guide to Conducting Sample Surveys

YOUR GOAL To design and implement a sample survey and report your methods clearly.

Introduction

This chapter is a continuation of Chapter 4 where we introduced some basic concepts of survey research so that you could plan a survey. The purpose of this chapter is to provide more detailed steps in actually implementing the survey and providing some basic analysis of the results. The format for a comprehensive report of a survey study is described in the previous chapter.

The checklist below is a summary of Chapter 4 as well as the procedures on data collection and analysis provided in this chapter. Carefully read the entire checklist before reviewing Chapter 4 and reading the rest of this chapter.

Check-List of Tasks Necessary for Conducting a Sample Survey

I. Determine what your client wants.

1.1 Identify your client's goals.

1.2 Indicate how each piece of information will help achieve the client's goals.

1.3 Identify any others in addition to your client who will be able to use the information and how they will use it.

2. Identify your target population and how you will sample it.

2.1 Define precisely the target population that you will sample for your survey including location and size.

2.2 Indicate the size of the sample you plan to analyze, the approximate percentage this represents of the target population, and the 95 percent confidence interval.

2.3 Indicate how you will select the actual individuals who will be in your sample.

2.4 Indicate at least one of the key variables you will use, such as gender or age, to compare the characteristics of the sample with the population. Indicate why you have chosen this as the comparison variable.

3. Create a plan for conducting the survey.

3.1 Indicate how you will contact the individuals to gather information (e.g., face-to-face, telephone, or mail). Justify your decision.

3.2 Estimate and justify an expected response rate. Indicate how many people you expect to contact to achieve your desired number of respondents.

3.3 Schedule the dates for conducting the survey.

4. Draft the questionnaire.

4.1 Write an introductory script or cover letter.

4.2 Write some questions to gather information with which to compare your sample to the target population.

4.3 Write the closed-choice questions and the response categories.

4.4 List any open-ended questions and indicate how you will record and report the answers.

4.5 Have the draft reviewed by your client, representatives of the population, and knowledgeable readers before you conduct the pilot test.

5. Plan a pilot test of the survey.

5.1 Decide how many respondents you want for a pilot.

5.2 List what you expect to learn from the pilot.

5.3 Schedule when you will conduct and assess the pilot, and make any changes in the questionnaire.

5.4 Make needed changes in your questionnaire or approach to the respondent.

6. Plan data collection.

6.1 Estimate the number of questionnaires and other materials you will need.

6.2 Develop a detailed plan for administering questionnaires.

6.3 Monitor data collection, testing your results against schedule and adjust procedures as necessary.

7. Prepare a Summary of Frequencies

7.1 Collect all of the questionnaires.

7.2 Take a blank questionnaire and record with hash marks the responses of all the completed questionnaires.

7.3 Use a spreadsheet program to tabulate your responses if it is quicker than doing it by hand.

7.4 Take another blank questionnaire and write in the summary information.

If you have reviewed the checklist and if you have a draft of the survey using the guidelines provided in Chapter 4, you are ready to (1) plan a pilot test; (2) plan your data collection; and (3) prepare a summary of frequencies.

Task 1: Plan a Pilot Test

- Decide how many respondents you want for a pilot.
- List what you expect to learn from the pilot.
- Schedule when you will conduct the pilot.
- Make needed changes in your questionnaire or approach to the respondent.

Although you and your client may be pleased with the initial design of your questionnaire, it is important to test it on a small portion of the target population to ensure that the questions are clear and that the information you collect is what your client wants. Pilot test your survey on a group of five to 10 members of the target population. Select members who are as representative as possible. For example, if the population consists of a 50-50 male to female ratio, select your pilot group to reflect the same proportion. However, do not focus too much energy on an exact match. It is important to pilot test your questionnaire quickly so that you can use the results to revise it, if necessary. After you have collected and tabulated the data from the pilot test, review each of the previous tasks to determine whether revisions are necessary.

You should pay attention to the design of the questions themselves, especially to the following two concerns:

1. Does the respondent understand the questions as intended?

For example, when high school biology teachers were asked about the major problems they faced when teaching, the following choices were given:

poor test books   lack of lab equipment
poor student preparation   discipline

To the surprise of the surveyors, "discipline" was identified as the leading problem by more than 90 percent of the respondents. The surveyors were surprised because they used the word "discipline" to mean the "discipline of biology," whereas the teachers saw it as coping with unruly student behavior.

2. Is the information generated by the question what the client wanted?

For example, a question asked during a pilot test for the evaluation of the Teens Teaching Spanish program was:

Would you continue in this program if you had more time?
___Yes   ___No   ___Not Sure

Of the respondents, 75 percent answered "No," whereas 95 percent answered on a previous question that they had learned a lot from the program, and that they had enjoyed it. We found out that most of them answered "No" because they felt that they had learned as much Spanish as they thought they needed. The surveyors intended the question to determine whether the participants had a positive attitude about the program. Therefore, they added, *"If 'No' why not?"* to the question to see whether or not the "No" answer measured negative attitudes.

Task 2: Plan Data Collection

- Estimate the number of questionnaires and other materials you will need.

- Develop a detailed plan for administering questionnaires.

- Monitor data collection testing your results against schedule and adjust procedures as necessary.

These tasks require serious attention to detail and appreciation of the power of Murphy's Law: "What Can Go Wrong, Will Go Wrong." Check to make sure that the required number of questionnaires is produced on time. A mistake that sometimes occurs is that the pages for a multi-page questionnaire are collated in the wrong order. Do not assume those who are administering the questionnaire will be as concerned about meeting deadlines and collecting responses as you are. Maintain a checklist that requires you to double-check with those responsible for distributing and collecting or mailing and receiving the questionnaires. Establish target dates when you expect to have 25%, 50%, 75%, and 100% of the questionnaires returned. Remember the 80-20 rule: in this case, it means that you will receive 80 percent of the questionnaires within the first 20 percent of the time allocated while the last 20 percent will be received very slowly. Determine a realistic cut-off date and don't accept any questionnaires after that date unless your response rate is far below what you expected. For telephone surveys, start early. Try a variety of days of the week and times of the day, and be ready for many disconnected telephones and quick hang-ups. Don't call too late, too early, or at dinnertime. If a respondent is not available, or you reach an answering machine, attempt to contact them at least two more times.

Task 3: Prepare a Summary of Frequencies

- Collect all of the questionnaires.
- Take a blank questionnaire and record with hash marks the responses of all the completed questionnaires.
- Take another blank questionnaire and write in the summary information.
- Use a spreadsheet program to tabulate your responses if it is quicker than doing it by hand.

Although you will probably want to prepare a formal report on the findings of your survey, you will always need to do a preliminary analysis of the frequencies of responses to each question. The format shown in this section is easy to prepare and can be used to show your client the initial results. This preliminary analysis will help you to decide what kinds of graphs and tables, as well as statistics, you might want to use.

To illustrate, let's assume that you have asked 50 people to answer the following as part of a questionnaire:

1. What is your gender?
   ___Male   ___Female

2. Did you wear a seat belt the last time you drove a car?
   ___Yes ___No ___Don't Know

3.   Briefly describe what you do when a passenger in a car you are driving refuses to wear a seat belt.

After collecting the 50 completed questionnaires, take a blank questionnaire on which to record the information. After five questionnaires, the one on which you were recording might look like this:

1.   What is your gender? _///_ Male _//_ Female

2.   Did you wear a seat belt the last time you drove a car?
     _//_ Yes   _//_ No   _/_ Don't Know

3.   Briefly describe what you do when a passenger in a car you are driving refuses to wear a seat belt.
     _//_ Nothing
     _//_ No Answer
     _/_ Don't start until they buckle up

Once your recording was done, you would copy the results on another blank questionnaire, resulting in something like this:

1.   What is your gender? Male (28) Female (22)

2.   Did you wear a seat belt the last time you drove a car?
     ____Yes (35)   ____No (10)   ____Don't Know (5)

3.   Briefly describe what you do when a passenger in a car you are driving refuses to use a seat belt.
     ____Nothing (21)
     ____Give reasons why important (12)
     ____Don't start until they buckle up (9)
     ____No answer (8)

If you have only a few questionnaires to analyze, you can do your tabulations by hand. For larger surveys, you should use a spreadsheet or database program to tabulate the responses. When tabulating by hand, follow the steps above.

Chapter 16

Quantitative Skills

YOUR GOAL   To explore basic quantitative analysis tools in policy research.

Introduction

In this chapter, you will be introduced to the skills necessary to interpret conditions relevant to public policy using statistical analysis.

The making and analyzing of policy are increasingly dependent upon the use of numbers and graphs. We use numbers in almost every aspect of communication. Our favorite sports team is described as "Number I." Academic performance is described by the Grade Point Average (GPA).

Numbers and graphs can convey an idea in a form that is both interesting and clear. Once you learn the basics of presentation, you will find that with numbers and graphs, you can make an argument more effectively than with words alone.

People collect and interpret numerical data when they analyze public policy issues for two primary reasons:

1. Numbers are helpful in acquiring a general grasp of factors affecting public policy issues.

2. Numbers can provide a precise statement about those factors. Only by the use of numbers can precise comparisons be made between different locations, periods of time, and target populations.

> **Statement 1: This year's unemployment is worse than last year's unemployment.**
>
> **Statement 2: Unemployment in New York State is 6.2 percent this year, compared to 5.5 percent last year.**

Consider the two statements in the box above. The second statement is preferable to the first statement because it communicates both a general picture of social conditions and a precise measure. It indicates that unemployment is higher this year than last and by how much. It also indicates the geographical area to which the statement applies.

Numbers and graphs can be used in all areas of public policy analysis, but they are most extensively used to measure societal conditions. Figure 16.1 presents examples of data that might be found in each of the three components of public policy issues described in Chapter 1.

The use of numbers and graphs in public policy analysis requires the completion of three tasks:

1. Selecting the most appropriate numerical information available.

2. Selecting the most appropriate type of analysis and display.

3. Making an interpretation that relates the analysis and display to the public policy.

Figure 16.1: Examples of numerical data used to describe the components of public policy issues

Societal Conditions	Players	Public Policies
Unemployment	Survey of attitudes of legislators	Government expenditure
Inflation		
Economic growth	Political contributions received	Tax rates
Tax payments		
Traffic fatalities	Legislative voting records	Minimum wage
Drug use		
School attendance	Patterns of party representation	Social Security benefits

Interpreting numerical information means explaining the reasons behind the information and drawing an inference about the information. More specifically, interpretation means providing the following:

- Summarizing the main point of what the numbers say, frequently presented as a headline above the table or graph.

- Explaining the reasons for the conditions shown by the numbers.

- Drawing conclusions from the numbers. Depending on your purpose, any conclusion may take one or more of several forms: Evidence for the existence and magnitude of a societal problem; an underlying factor contributing to the existence of a societal problem; an evaluation of the effects of previous policies on a societal problem; or the history and forecast of a societal problem for which you are proposing a policy solution.

The rest of this chapter describes and illustrates some additional principles of using tables and graphs in analyzing policy. It covers the following topics:

1. Scaling numbers

2. Presenting data with tables

3. Presenting data with bar graphs

4. Using trend lines

5. Displaying components with pie charts

6. Describing differences with percentages

7. Comparing two groups

1. Scaling Numbers

Whenever you use numbers in a table or graph, report them in such a way that they are easy to compare and interpret. It is usually better to report comparable numbers, such as percentages or per capita rates, rather than raw numbers. Making the numbers comparable is called scaling.

In many cases, converting raw numbers to percentages is enough to make them easy to interpret. For example, suppose 2,514 employees work in a state environmental agency. Of these employees, 274 are assigned to enforcement of illegal toxic dumping. The percentage of those assigned to enforcement is:

$$\frac{274}{2,514} = .10899 \text{ (rounded)} \times 100 = 10.9\%$$

Figure 16.2: Total traffic deaths in selected states, 1985

State	Deaths
California	4,999
New York	2,065
Alabama	939
Massachusetts	663
New Mexico	497

Source: National Safety Council. (1986). *The world almanac and book of facts.* New York: Newspaper Enterprise Association. p. 781.

A percentage is one form of a "rate," which means the number of things per some other number. Examples of commonly used rates are 100, 1,000, or some other multiple of 10. A percentage is a rate per 100. Another example of a rate is infant mortality, which is calculated as the number of infant deaths per 1,000 live births. Another form of a rate is the difference between raw numbers and those reported in a more appropriate scale. The table above shows the number of traffic deaths in a selected group of states.

Does this mean that California and New York are the most dangerous places to drive, while Alabama, Massachusetts, and New Mexico are the safest? Not necessarily. Part of the reason that California and New York have many traffic deaths and that Alabama, Massachusetts, and New Mexico have few traffic deaths may be the difference in the number of miles driven in each state. It is better to report the traffic death rate, that is, the number of deaths divided by the number of miles driven in each state. The usual method of reporting automobile traffic death rate is the number of deaths for each 100 million miles driven. Since very high numbers of miles are driven in California and New York, their high traffic death totals are divided by large numbers, which tends to lower their death rate. On the other hand, Alabama and New Mexico have fewer drivers and fewer roads, so their traffic death totals are divided by a smaller number, making their death rate higher. What about Massachusetts? It has a fairly low death total; it also has a high number of miles driven. Where will it rank when its traffic death total is divided by the miles driven in the state?

The answer is given in Figure 16.3 on the next page, where the states are listed according to their traffic death rate—total traffic deaths per 100 million miles driven.

In the figure, the rankings are quite different. New Mexico and Alabama have the highest death rates, California and New York are in the middle, and Massachusetts has the lowest traffic death rate.

State	Deaths per 100 Million Miles Driven
New Mexico	4.3
Alabama	3.1
California	2.9
New York	2.4
Massachusetts	1.7

Source: National Safety Council. (1986). *The world almanac and book of facts.* New York: Newspaper Enterprise Association. p. 781.

The scale you use depends on the kind of information you are reporting. Often percentages are used, which means that each number is divided by the same total. This shows what fraction each number represents of the entire total. Examples of such presentations include budget figures, racial composition of a city, and the number of males and females in particular occupational groups.

Another common way of presenting numbers is on a per capita basis, in which each number is divided by the population of the unit (for example, school, city, or state) being reported. Examples include crime rates in different neighborhoods of a city and income levels in different cities. Sometimes, if numbers involved are quite small, the figure is reported not in terms of the number of people but in terms of 100 or 1,000 people. Some commonly used figures are reported as percentages, such as unemployment rates, which means the number of unemployed individuals per 100 people in the labor force looking for work.

To convert raw numbers to numbers that can be easily compared, do the following:

1. Decide if the raw number is adequate without making some conversion. This is possible in some rare instances. If not, go to step 2.

    For the example of traffic deaths, the raw numbers for traffic deaths are shown below.

California	4,999
Alabama	939
New York	2,065
New Mexico	497
Massachusetts	663

2. Choose the unit that should be divided into the raw number to allow for comparisons. As noted above, you may want to use the total which would give you a percentage or per capita figure.

For the example of traffic deaths, the unit chosen, 100 million miles traveled, is shown below.

California	1,724
Alabama	303
New York	860
New Mexico	116
Massachusetts	390

3. Divide the raw number by the unit number. Clearly label the number and provide a specific description of the source.

For the example on traffic deaths, the division and scaled numbers, total traffic deaths per 100 million miles traveled, are shown below.

California $\dfrac{4,999}{1,724}$ = 2.9

Alabama $\dfrac{939}{303}$ = 3.1

New York $\dfrac{2,065}{860}$ = 2.4

New Mexico $\dfrac{497}{116}$ = 4.3

Massachusetts $\dfrac{663}{390}$ = 1.7

Source: National Safety Council. (1986). *The world almanac and book of facts.* New York: Newspaper Enterprise Association. p. 781.

2. Presenting Data with Tables

Data must be presented in a form that is both interesting and clear. Stringing numbers together in a text does not accomplish either of these goals. For example, consider the following hypothetical example:

A recent study, "Committee for the Aging: Research and Education" (CARE) indicates that, in 1920, the percentage of the United States population 60 years of age and over was 6%; in 1940, the percentage was 8%; in 1960, it was 13%; in 1980, it was 15%; and in 2000, it is forecast to be 20%.

Figure 16.4: From 1920-2000 the percent of the United States population at least 60 years of age, is expected to grow to one-fifth of the total population.

Year	Percentage
1920	6%
1940	8%
1960	13%
1980	15%
2000f	20%

Source: Committee for the Aging: Research and Education. (1985). New York: CARE.

Such information is difficult to understand presented in this way. If arranged in a table, as above, it is much easier to read. Note the "f" at the end of the year 2000 indicates the figure for that year is a forecast.

Tables are a widely used and accepted means of organizing small sets of data for rapid visualization and understanding. A table requires:

- A title which clearly explains its nature or indicates its main point.

- Data elements carefully listed in some logical order (by time, in rank order, or some other sequence) under headings which clearly specify units of measurement.

- Documentation of the data source. Just listing the organization issuing the information is not adequate. Each source must have the author or organization if there is one, the title of the document or website, and the date of publication.

3. Presenting Data with Bar Graphs

An even more striking way of presenting data is to use a bar graph, which is a series of parallel bars (or similar markings) placed either vertically or horizontally to indicate totals or percentages. In the construction of a bar graph, the length of the bars and the space between them should be consistent and allow for clear visual inspection. Normally, a vertical (or y) axis is drawn with the scale placed alongside, while the horizontal (or x) axis is labeled with what units are being compared or measured. Bar graphs should be used any time you want to compare two or more units (for example: states, cities, years, or sub-groups of a population).

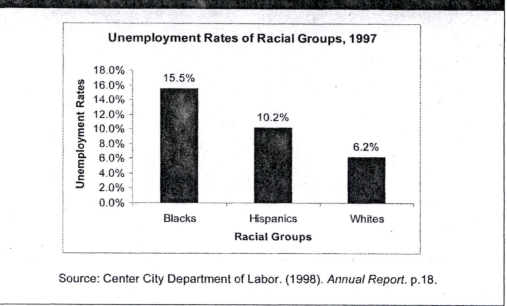

Figure 16.5: In 1997, African Americans and Hispanics had higher unemployment rates in Center City

Unemployment Rates of Racial Groups, 1997

Source: Center City Department of Labor. (1998). *Annual Report*. p.18.

Figure 16.5 provides information on the rate of unemployment among different segments of the population for the first quarter of 1997 in a hypothetical city. Each bar represents a different segment of the employable population with the actual rate printed at the top of the bar. The height of the bars allows the reader to see the difference in unemployment of different racial groups.

4. Using Trend Lines

A trend line is a common form of graph. The trend line is derived from plotting time in years, months, or days on the x-axis (horizontal), and plotting the factor which is changing over time on the y-axis (vertical). This type of graph shows the progress of that which is on the y-axis over time. The trend can also be projected into the future. In Figure 16.6 on the next page, the forecast data is represented by a different symbol. This type of display is useful in monitoring and forecasting social conditions. Figure 16.6 shows the trend from 1990 projected through 2000 on the number of deaths expected from AIDS in a hypothetical city.

5. Displaying Components with Pie Charts

A pie chart can be used to show how the component parts of a total are divided. The distribution of government spending or the ethnic composition of a political party are examples of subjects that can be displayed using this technique. To construct a pie chart, remember that the total of 100 percent is described by a circle

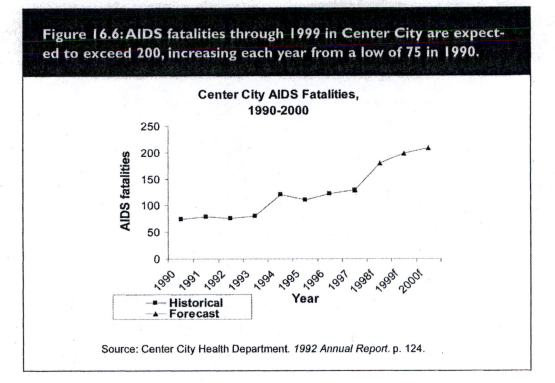

Figure 16.6: AIDS fatalities through 1999 in Center City are expected to exceed 200, increasing each year from a low of 75 in 1990.

Center City AIDS Fatalities, 1990-2000

AIDS fatalities

- ■ Historical
- ▲ Forecast

Year

Source: Center City Health Department. *1992 Annual Report.* p. 124.

of 360 degrees. Thus, each percentage point is equal to an arc of 3.6 degrees. To illustrate, we will construct a pie chart to show the distribution of people over 60 years of age in a hypothetical city as outlined in Figure 16.7. Each percent figure in the table below is multiplied by 3.6 degrees to determine the size of the arc that must be drawn for each segment of the pie.

If necessary, use a protractor to measure the necessary degrees on the circle. Each segment should be labeled with both a name and a percent. Labels may go either inside or outside the circle. Labels should be placed outside if the sections are especially narrow. As illustrated in Figure 16.8 on the next page, the pie chart can be an effective technique for the visual display of data. A pie chart is not, however, appropriate for all displays. Pie charts containing more than eight segments or con-

Figure 16.7: Age distribution of residents age 60 and above

Age Group	Percent				Arc (degrees)
60—64 years	29.7	x	3.6	=	106.92
65—74	43.6	x	3.6	=	156.96
75—84	21.1	x	3.6	=	75.96
85 and older	5.6	x	3.6	=	20.16
Total	**100.00**				**360.00**

Figure 16.8: About one-fourth of Center City's residents over age 60 are among the "Very Old"—75 years and older

Age Distribution of Residents Age 60 and Above, Center City, 1992

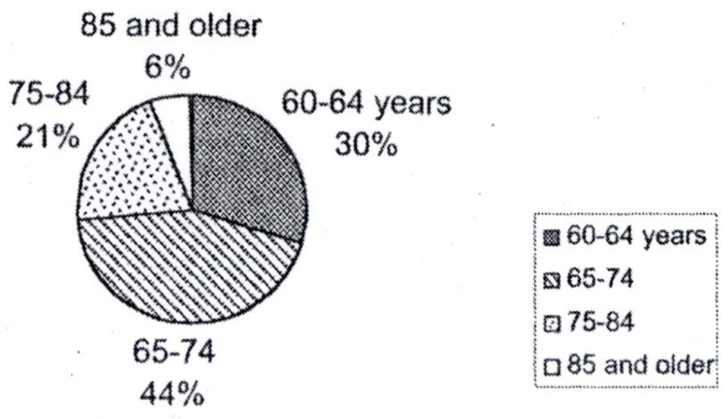

85 and older
6%

75-84
21%

60-64 years
30%

65-74
44%

Legend:
- 60-64 years
- 65-74
- 75-84
- 85 and older

Source: Committee for the Aging: Research and Education. (1992). *The needs of the very elderly.* p. 5.

taining several segments with very small arcs (less than 5 percent) are difficult to label and interpret.

6. Describing Differences with Percentages

A percentage difference is a simple but powerful tool for comparing two sets of numbers. You may want to determine the differences between estimated and actual budget figures or between one year's crime rate and another's. Percentages are used to determine precise differences in three ways:

1. Comparison of estimated to actual. For example, the original estimate of the federal budget deficit for 1983 was $113.65 billion, but the actual deficit was $195.4 billion. The actual figure was 73 percent higher than the estimate.

2. Comparison between numbers for the same period of time. For example, in 1986, the population of the U.S.S.R. was 279.5 million, and the population of the U.S. was 241.6 million. The population of the U.S.S.R. was 15.7 percent larger than the U.S. population.

3. Comparison between two periods of time. For example, the number of felonies in New York City was 637,451 in 1981, while the number fell to 538,051 in 1984. The number of felonies declined 16 percent between 1981 and 1984.

Here is the procedure for calculating percent differences:

New Figure - Original Figure   x   100   =   **Percent Difference**
   Original Figure

For example (from point 3, above):

1984 Felonies - 1981 Felonies   x   100   =   **Percent Difference**
   1981 Felonies

$$\frac{538,051 - 637,451}{637,451} = \frac{-99,400}{637,451} = -.1559 \times \underline{100} = -16\%$$

If you are comparing two numbers in the same time period, you may use either one as the "new figure" and the other as the "original figure."

One question you must answer when comparing percentages is "How big is big enough to make a difference?" Suppose, for example, you conduct a survey of two different high schools to find out how many seniors are planning to attend college. Suppose in one school 87 percent plan to go to college, and in the other school 88 percent plan to attend college. With numbers so close, it would not make sense to conclude that the two schools differ significantly regarding college attendance. But what if the two figures were 87 percent and 89 percent? Or 87 percent and 92 percent? Or 87 percent and 97 percent? At what point would you be justified in saying the two schools were significantly different?

Fortunately, statisticians have developed a systematic procedure for making such conclusions. It is based on how many individuals are in each of the two groups being compared, as well as the magnitude of the percent difference between the two groups. This procedure is summarized in Figure 16.9 on the next page. To use the table, find the size of one of your groups (either one) somewhere down the row of the table. If the group size is between numbers on the row of the table, use the smaller number. Then find the appropriate column based on the size of the other group (again, using the smaller number if the actual group size is between numbers shown on the columns). At the intersection of the row corresponding to the size of the first group and the column corresponding to the size of the second group is a number. That number tells you how big the percentages between two groups must be before concluding that there is a significant difference. The table is based on a confidence interval of 95 percent. In other words, the table will give correct results in 95 out of 100 cases.

Figure 16.9: Minimum difference in percentage points required to conclude that there is a statistically significant difference between two groups of different sizes (with 95% confidence).

One Group is at Least	The Other Group is at Least:									
	30	50	90	150	300	600	1000	1500	2000	3000
30	25	23	21	20	19	19	19	19	19	18
50	23	20	18	16	15	15	15	15	15	14
90	21	18	15	14	12	12	11	11	11	11
150	20	16	14	12	10	9	9	9	9	9
300	19	15	12	10	8	7	7	7	7	6
600	19	15	12	9	7	6	6	5	5	5
1000	19	15	11	9	7	6	5	4	4	4
1500	19	15	11	9	7	5	4	4	4	4
2000	19	15	11	9	7	5	4	4	4	3
3000	18	14	11	9	6	5	4	4	3	3

To illustrate how to use the table, consider the sample of the two schools mentioned above. The table tells us that a difference of one or two percentage points (87% to 88%, or 87% to 89%, for example) would not be significant even if the size of the groups surveyed in the two schools consisted of 3,000 students each. Even with such huge groups, a difference of at least 3 percentage points would be required to conclude that a significant difference existed. The table also shows that even a difference of 10 percentage points (87% to 97%, for example) should not be considered significant unless one of the groups consisted of at least 150 students and the other group consisted of at least 300 students. From this table, you can see why it is important to obtain large samples. Unless you have samples of well more than 100, you must obtain huge differences in percentage points to conclude a difference between groups. If the size of either or both of your groups does not exactly match the table, use the next smaller figure on the table. This is a conservative decision, which you should always follow in statistical procedures.

7. Comparing Two Groups

Many times in analyzing societal conditions it is important to see how two groups can be compared with one another with respect to an opinion, behavior, or how they have been affected by previous policies. Here, for example, are some questions that policy analysts may want answered:

- How do athletes and non-athletes in a high school differ with respect to a proposed "No pass, no play" policy concerning athletic eligibility?

- How do parents and students in a survey differ with respect to support for a proposed environmental policy?

- How do two different cities differ with respect to their crime rates?

A properly constructed table can help provide answers to these questions. Such a table is a cross-tabulation of two different variables.

For example, consider the first question above, how athletes and non-athletes differ with respect to a proposed "No pass, no play" policy. Assume that a survey has been conducted at a high school, that the sample was randomly selected according to the guidelines in Chapters 4 and 15, and that the sample contains both athletes and non-athletes. Suppose that one of the survey questions was:

"What is your attitude regarding the proposed rule under which any school athlete who is not passing in all courses will be ineligible to compete for the school?: __ AGREE __ DISAGREE"

Further assume that of 300 students surveyed, 90 were athletes and 210 were non-athletes. Of the 90 athletes, 30 agreed with the policy and 60 disagreed. Of the 210 non-athletes, 160 students agreed with the policy and 50 disagreed.

These results can be clearly shown in a table as follows, in which the two different groups (athletes vs. non-athletes) are used to form the vertical columns, and the answers are shown in the horizontal rows.

Figure 16.10: Athletes and non-athletes differ significantly regarding the proposed "No Pass, No Play" policy.

Attitude Toward "No Pass, No Play"	Type of Student		
	Athlete	Non-Athlete	TOTAL
Agree	30 (33%)	160 (76%)	90 (63%)
Disagree	60 (67%)	50 (24%)	110 (36%)
TOTAL	90 (30%)	210 (70%)	300 (100%)

(Percentages may not add to 100% because of rounding)

Source: Student Survey, Central High School, Fall semester.

This table conveys a great deal of information when used with the appropriate tables and statistics.

1. The marginal totals and percentages to the right indicate the overall support for the proposed policy: 63% agree and 36% disagree. Note that 63% + 36% does not add to exactly 100% because of rounding. It is quite common, and no cause for concern, to have rounded percentages that should add to 100% actually add to 99% or 101%.

2. The marginal totals and percentages along the bottom row indicate the distribution of the sample: 70% non-athletes and 30% athletes. This figure might be used to check the representatives of the sample. Since Figure 4.1 (page 43) tells us that a sample of 300 should have a target population of between 24% and 36% athletes (30% +/- 6%), we could check school records to see if the number of athletes was actually within that range. If the percentage of athletes was within that range, this would be evidence that our sampling procedure gave us a representative sample. If it turned out that there were fewer than 24% athletes or more than 36%, this would be a warning that our sampling was not actually as representative as we thought and that we had somehow introduced bias into the sampling process.

3. The column percentages comparing the agreement and disagreement of the two groups make clear how sharply the athletes and non-athletes differ on the question of the policy. As Figure 16.9 in this chapter shows, when you have one group of 30 (the number of athletes who agree with the policy) and another group of 90 (the number of non-athletes who agree), a difference of at least 21 percentage points is required to be 95% confident that there is a statistically significant difference between the two groups. The difference in the table is 43 percentage points (76—the percentage of non-athletes agreeing, minus 33—the percentage of athletes agreeing.) Since the 43 percentage points are much higher than the 21 point minimum in the table, we can say with 95 percent confidence that athletes and non-athletes clearly differ on the policy.

In other cases, the figures you present may be averages or rates rather than percentages. For example, you might compare crime rates in two different communities or average tax rates in two different school districts. The principle is the same, using the groups to define the columns and presenting comparable numbers in each row.

Examining the side-by-side column percentages is a quick way to compare groups, especially when they are of different sizes. This is why it is necessary to present not just totals but also percentages or other comparable figures. Statistical procedures, which are not covered in this chapter, exist for determining when figures other than percentages are large enough to conclude that the two groups are significantly different. For this reason, it is preferable to convert numbers to percentages, and then use the table of minimum required percentage point differences.

References

Boyer, E. (1987). *College: The undergraduate experience in America*. New York: Harper & Row.

Boyer, E. (1990). *Scholarship reconsidered*. New York: The Carnegie Foundation for the Advancement of Teaching.

Coplin, W. (2003). *10 things employers want you to learn in college*. Berkeley, CA: Ten Speed Press.

Coplin, W., & Dwyer, C. (2000). *Does your government measure up?: Basic tools for local officials and citizens*. Syracuse, NY: Syracuse University Press.

Mandela, N. (1995). *Long walk to freedom: The autobiography of Nelson Mandela*. New York: Back Bay Books.

O' Sullivan, E., & Rassel, G. (1994). *Research methods for public administrators*. White Plains, NY: Longmans.

Osborne, D., & Gaebler, T. (1993). *Reinventing government: How the entrepreneurial spirit is transforming the public sector*. New York: Plume.